# Battleground E...

## DIE

With the continued expansion of the Battleground series a **Battleground Series Club** has been formed to benefit the reader. The purpose of the Club is to keep members informed of new titles and to offer many other reader-benefits. Membership is free and by registering an interest you can help us predict print runs and thus assist us in maintaining the quality and prices at their present levels.

Please call the office 01226 734555, or send your name and address along with a request for more information to:

**Battleground Series Club** Pen & Sword Books Ltd,
47 Church Street, Barnsley, South Yorkshire S70 2AS

# Battleground Europe
## DIEPPE

# THE DIEPPE RAID
## 2nd Canadian Division

Tim Saunders

Pen & Sword
**MILITARY**

*This book is dedicated to my wife Kate with love.*

First published in Great Britain in 2005 by
Pen & Sword Military
an imprint of
Pen & Sword Books Ltd
47 Church Street
Barnsley
South Yorkshire
S70 2AS

**ISBN 1 84415 245 6**

A CIP catalogue record for this book is
available from the British Library

Typeset in Palatino

Printed and bound in the United Kingdom by CPI

Pen & Sword Books Ltd incorporates the Imprints of Pen & Sword Aviation,Pen
& Sword Maritime, Pen & Sword Military, Wharncliffe Local History, Pen and
Sword Select, Pen and Sword Military Classics and Leo Cooper.
For a complete list of Pen & Sword titles, please contact
Pen & Sword Books Limited
47 Church Street, Barnsley, South Yorkshire, S70 2AS, England
E-mail: enquiries@pen-and-sword.co.uk
Website: www.pen-and-sword.co.uk

# CONTENTS

Wounded being taken aborad a destroyer during the evacuation.

# INTRODUCTION

There are two passages of text that to my mind sum up the whole context of the Dieppe raid. The first is a US newspaper commentary on the heroism of fellow North Americans and the second are the words of an experienced Canadian soldier in the immediate aftermath of Operation Jubilee. The *New York Times* 19 August 1943 wrote:

> *'Someday there will be two spots on the French coast sacred to the British and their Allies. One will be Dunkirk where Britain was saved because a beaten army would not surrender.*
>
> *'The other will be Dieppe, where brave men died without hope for the sake of proving that there is a wrong way to invade. They will have their share of glory when the right way is tried.'*

The second piece is by Captain Denis Whitaker of the Royal Hamilton Light Infantry who recorded how Combined Operation's Headquarters (COHQ) summoned him after the raid:

> *'The debriefing had begun when I finally got to London. I recognized the Dieppe military commander, Major General Roberts – his face bore a gaunt stricken look... the two men beside Admiral Mountbatten were the naval and air commanders of the operation...*
>
> *'General Roberts was finishing his reports. "I am inclined to question whether tactical surprise was achieved... It is evident that the German gun crews were*

*standing by with all defence posts manned when the first wave of troops came in."*

*'Mountbatten shrugged of the comments impatiently. "You have to take into account that a state of alert was normal at dawn, and that the conditions of weather and tide might have increased the state of alert".*

*'I stood up. My mind reeled. So surprise had never been possible! "Sir. I landed on the main beach. When I interrogated a German prisoner, he boasted, we have been waiting for you for a week.'*

*'Sit down, Captain Whitaker. I do not believe the enemy was forewarned. I want constructive comments – not excuses."'*

From these two quotes, it can be seen that almost immediately, the scale of the sacrifice, amongst Canadian and British sailors, soldiers and airmen, combined with the painful examination of military failure, led to the Dieppe Raid's enduring fascination. However, as it is the role of the **Battleground** series to concentrate on the conduct of the fighting, this book can only dedicate a modest amount of space to the main features of the controversial background to the raid. This should not represent too much of a hardship for readers, as there are literally yards of books that almost exclusively examine the political, strategic and intelligence background to Operation Jubilee. Most are not shy at apportioning blame. A bibliography of published sources and other useful Dieppe books, including a number of other Pen and Sword titles, is at the end of this volume.

British readers should note that other than on first mention I have for the sake of economy of space dropped the Suffix 'of Canada' for the Black Watch and Cameron Highlanders. Though the British and Canadian regiments bearing these names had affiliations and a common Scottish heritage, they were very much separate organisations.

**'Nazi circles have tried desperately to prove that the Dieppe raid was unsuccessful. They have failed.'**
**So ran an editorial comment in the *Sunday Pictorial*, 6 September 1942.**

# CHAPTER ONE

# BACKGROUND AND PLANS

The sound of boots on the gravel of the beach and the rattle of small-arms fire echoed around the cliffs of Le Touquet, south of Boulogne. On the night of 23/24 June 1940, just weeks after the British Army had abandoned its weapons and equipment at Dunkirk, a small group of soldiers from that defeated army returned to raid the mainland of Europe. Operation Collar, mounted by the newly-formed special raiding force was just a pin-prick, killing only two members of the mighty *Wehrmacht* which was at the time sealing its victory over the French. However, such an action was exactly what Churchill had envisaged when he ordered a 'special raiding force' to be raised. He wrote:

> 'The completely defensive habit of mind, which has ruined the French, must not be allowed to ruin our initiative. Enterprises must be prepared with specially trained troops of the hunter class, who can develop a reign of terror first of all on the butcher-and-bolt policy.'

The Prime Minister had no illusions that small raids would do anything to tip the military balance. But with personal experience of how effective the Boer *Kommandos* had been in South Africa, he

A wartime PR photo used to promote the Commandos' activities.

appreciated the value for morale at home of commando raids, and also how many thousands of enemy troops would be tied down waiting for the next attack. Small raids reinforced the perception that Churchill was trying to create of an active resistance, and in a phrase familiar from the Great War, helped to 'maintain the offensive spirit.'

**Prime Minister Winston Churchill**

During the first year of the war, Commando Forces (with their famous green berets) grew in size, and mounted increasing numbers of raids, while British airborne forces developed military parachuting and trained for

**Lord Louis Mountbatten cousin of the King**

action. Veterans have frankly admitted that many of the first raids were 'amateurish'. But as the scale of raids grew, experience was gained, training techniques improved, and more of the raids were considered successful. In the first airborne raid, at Bruneval, vital German radar components were snatched. Raiding enemy-held coastlines, whether in France, the Mediterranean, or in the Far East, became a regular feature of British conduct of the war.

In the face of opposition from the three Services, Churchill formed a Combined Operations headquarters, under his personal attention, which grew from small beginnings with a limited advisory role into a major headquarters with a 'higher importance, a more positive function and a stronger staff'. Brigadier Lucas Phillips wrote:

> 'When the time came. . . we would have to fight for it, moreover, against seemingly impregnable coastal defences equipped with every modern preventive device and stratag. . . Technical problems of the most formidable magnitude confronted us, together with problems of tactics, transport and administration. "Co-operation" between the Services was not enough; there must be complete integration of thought, planning, experimentation and executive action.'

In March 1942, Churchill singled out 41-year-old Admiral Lord Louis Mountbatten as an inspiring and dynamic leader and

**Combined
Ops badge**

appointed him to the new post of Chief of Combined Operations. This not only put him at the head of an increasingly powerful independent-minded organisation but also gave him membership of the Chiefs of Staffs' Committee.

### The Situation in 1942

1942 ended with the 'turn of the tide,' following General Montgomery's victory at El Alamein, but in the first half of the year, without a doubt, the Allied prospects were unremittingly bad. Conversely, the Axis Powers were reaching their zenith. At home in the UK, the British people suffered the privations of rationing and a shortage of just about every commodity, as the *Kriegsmarine's* U-boat wolf packs unrelentingly attacked the convoys of merchantmen that represented Britain's lifeline to survival. On the battlefield, British and Commonwealth troops fighting in the deserts of North Africa were again being driven back by Rommel's *Afrika Korps*. Meanwhile, in the Far East, the Americans were still feeling the shock of their immense naval losses at Pearl Harbour, and were struggling to contain the Japanese forces who occupied island after island, including the Philippines, as they spread across the Pacific towards Australia. In February, the Japanese had seized Singapore and were advancing north through Burma towards India. Rangoon fell in early March and Mandalay in mid-April, sending the British and Chinese Armies retreating to the north. On the Eastern Front, military affairs were also going badly: despite a Russian counter-offensive, the Germans held their ground, and by May, the Russians were being pushed back by the *Wehrmacht* counter-offensive. In the spring of 1942, the immediate outlook for the Allies' was bleak.

**Joseph Stalin demanded
action in the West**

However, it was on the Eastern Front where the situation was most dangerous. Here, the *Wehrmacht* and the Red Army, together numbering millions of men, were pitted against each other in a titanic struggle to the death. The Russians, who had committed all in their spring offensive, were withdrawing in the face of a German thrust through the Caucasus Mountains

**German infantry advancing on Stalingrad in the summer of 1942**

toward Sevastopol. There seemed to be no way of halting the *Wehrmacht*. In consequence, Stalin demanded that the leaders of the Western Allies take action in the west to reduce pressure on his armies. He insisted that there was an imminent danger of the Red Army collapsing. Such a Russian military collapse was a real possibility, and would have had catastrophic effect on the Allied war effort, by releasing whole armies of Germans for employment elsewhere.

Russia's demands were strongly supported by the Americans, even though they themselves were unable at the time to provide significant material support, or troops, for an offensive in the West. Among senior American military and naval leaders, there was significant agitation toward concentrating their efforts in the Pacific against the Japanese. This pressure would prevail unless an offensive in the West was developed and executed within the short term. In both Britain and America, the public also agitated for offensive action to support the beleaguered Russians. During April 1942, mass rallies in both Trafalgar Square in London and Madison Square Gardens in New York called for 'a second front now!'

With pressure mounting at home and from across the Atlantic, Churchill and the British Chiefs of Staff were forced to develop plans for an offensive operation in the West. Proposals ranged from the grandiose but hopelessly unsustainable Operation Sledgehammer (the formation of a lodgement on the Cherbourg Peninsular) to more modest affairs. Whatever the scale of the operation, it was intended either to draw German divisions from the Russian front or at least to fix their existing divisions in place in the west, thus preventing them from reinforcing the Eastern Front. In pursuing this goal, Churchill stated that 'we should not hesitate to put into effect this year any sound and sensible plan to do more to draw the weight off Russia'. As the spring slipped into summer, pressure remained on the British to take action. It is recorded in the Official History *Grand Strategy* series that:

> *'Mountbatten also had a long conversation on 9th June with the President. Mr Roosevelt said he "wished to remind the Prime Minister of the agreement reached last time he was in Washington, that in the event of things going badly for the Russians this summer, a sacrifice landing would be carried out in France to assist them."'*

However, despite laudable aims to relieve pressure on the Russians, the Allies lacked the ability to project and sustain combat power across the English Channel. It is noted in *Grand Strategy* Volume III that,

> *'... the limiting factor as regards both the size of the force and the date was the lack of suitable shipping, especially tank-landing craft.*

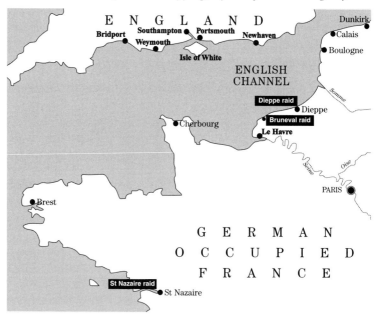

**HMS *Campbeltown* rammed into the St Nazaire dock gates before she exploded.**

> *Even if the initial assault succeeded, we should not have the craft to maintain it over the beaches in the absence of a port, and the ports of Calais and Boulogne were almost certain to be blocked.'*

It was against this menacing strategic background, with a lack of resources, and mounting pressure for action on mainland Europe, that the Dieppe raid was planned and executed. However, the strategic necessity of relieving pressure on the Russians was not the only factor at work.

Combined Operations Headquarters's (COHQ) star was in the ascendancy following the successful Commando attack on the port facilities of St Nazaire. Despite the seventy-nine percent casualties suffered at St Nazaire, the operation, overseen by Captain John Hughes-Hallet RN, blew the sea lock gates in a heavily defended port and was considered to be a success. It denied the German battleship *Tirpitz* the only dock on the Atlantic Coast capable of taking her. For operations against Allied North Atlantic convoys, *Tirpitz* was thus forced to operate from disadvantageous bases among the Norwegian fjords.

The raid's success against a strategically important target enabled Admiral Mountbatten, with a team of highly competent and ambitious young officers that he had gathered around him, to advance larger and more sophisticated raids on the enemy-held coast of France. The COHQ planners' next step was logically to mount a raid that combined significant forces from the Royal Navy, the Army and the Air Force in an ambitious undertaking. The port of Dieppe was to be their target. Unlike Bruneval or St Nazaire, there was no single objective of overwhelming strategic importance: this confirms that the Dieppe raid was part of a pattern of increasingly larger raids, and that Combined Operations was entering the phase of preparations to return to battle with the Germans on mainland Europe. In short, the raid was an experiment in landing techniques, but it also had elements of strategic necessity, *vis à vis* the Russians as well as satisfying the ambitions of a new and favoured headquarters and its commander.

## Dieppe

After the demise of Operation Sledgehammer, the COHQ Targeting Committee selected seven ports for consideration for a raid. All within the limited range of Allied fighters and fighter-bombers at this stage of the war. Of these ports along France's Channel Coast, Dieppe was one of a group of relatively lightly defended potential targets, and at sixty-five miles south of Newhaven, it was within the Allied air umbrella. Even so, Churchill continued to advance numerous offensive schemes. The Chief of Imperial General Staff

**Field Marshal Alanbrook**

(CIGS) Field Marshal Alanbrooke confided in exasperation to his diary, after a three-hour session with the Prime Minister:

'This meeting with Winston was typical of many others, when all difficulties were brushed aside and many unpleasant realities, such as resources available, were scrupulously avoided. He was carried away with optimism, and established lodgements all round the coast from Calais to Bordeaux with little regard to strength and landing facilities.'

One of CIGS's roles was to fend off the wilder ideas that emanated from Downing Street, other ministries and HQs, and to focus the underlying enthusiasm. Dieppe was only finally selected by Combined Operations as their next major target, however, after considerable debate. The planners' underlying purposes were, according to the

Portsmouth
Southampton

Newhaven

Official History *Grand Strategy*,

> '...to test the German coast defences and discover what resistance would have to be met in the endeavour to seize a port. It was hoped also to inflict heavy wastage on the German Air Force and thereby give some relief to the Russians.'

## Topography

The Combined Operations report, issued in October 1942, described Dieppe in the following terms:

> 'The port and town of Dieppe are situated in the bight between Boulogne and Fecamp on the north coast of France. The main part of the town is on the west side of the harbour at the mouth of the valley through which flows the river d'Arques.'

The report goes on to describe the access channel into the port, the outer or Avant Port, and the inner basin, its facilities and the various locks and bridges.

> 'The town lies in a gap about a mile wide in the cliffs at the mouth of the river... Dividing the town from the sea is a built-up promenade backed by a line of hotels and boarding houses. Between the promenade and the hotels lie lawns and gardens about 1,200 yards long and 150 yards wide. They are enclosed on two sides by broad boulevards, the Boulevard Marechal Foch on the north and Boulevard de Verdun on the south. At the western end of the lawns is the Casino. Immediately behind the hotels, the Town Hall, and the Tobacco Factory, is the Old Town.'

To the east and west of the town, the chalk hills rise steeply from the suburbs, and in the eleven miles astride Dieppe, 'the coast consists of high cliffs, only accessible for landing in a few places.' Along this coast, the beaches were a narrow strip of stones and boulders, and apart from a few mouths of small river valleys, where there were small beaches, the exits up the cliff were up via narrow valleys or, in the worst case, up gullies. Planners were dubious about the possibility of landing tanks and vehicles on the small beaches at anything but high water, because of rocky ledges. Given the topography of the beaches, it was considered that:

> 'The landing must therefore take place above half tide. . . and these conditions required come round about ten days in each lunar month. A wind of not more than force 3, with no swell, is also essential, and this reduces the chance of bringing off an operation of this kind to two days a month in an average summer.'

## Operational Planning

'It's on' was Mountbatten's brief annotation to the Targeting Committee's report recom-mending Dieppe for the next major raid: on 4 April 1942, planning for what became known as Operation Rutter began. The COHQ report des-cribed Rutter's planning process, which was not without its difficulties:

*'It was early in April 1942 that the question of an attack on Dieppe was first examined by the Target Committee of Combined Operations Headquarters. About the middle of that month, the Planning Staff of that Headquarters began work on an outline plan of attack under the general direction of Captain J. Hughes Hallett R.N., who was subsequently the Naval Force Commander for the second attempt. It was realised at the outset, that, though intelligence reports showed that Dieppe was not very heavily defended, a town of its size could only be successfully raided if the number of troops used was considerable. It was estimated that as many as six battalions would be necessary. The question of giving them adequate support at once arose and the use of tanks was considered very early in the planning.'*

It was the issue of the deployment of tanks for the first time in a Combined Ops raid that largely defined the Dieppe concept of operations and the eventual plan.

A frontal assault was not at first contemplated by the Planning Staff. They thought that the best places for landings would be on each flank at Quiberville, some six miles to the west of Dieppe, and at Criel-sur-Mer, about double that distance to the east. At Quiberville, the beach was deemed suitable for tanks; once ashore they would only have to go a short distance towards the aerodrome of St Aubin and to the high ground to the south-west and west of the town, both of them suitable objectives of which the capture would secure Dieppe from the west. The main obstacles which the tanks would encounter would be the Rivers Saane and Scie.

A tank landing well to the east of Dieppe presented greater problems. 'The beach at Criel-sur-Mer... might not be particularly suitable for the landing of tanks, but at that time full information concerning it was lacking.' In addition, some planners thought that the tanks would be forced by the nature of the ground to take a route looping two or three miles inland. They thus 'would have to travel some twelve or fourteen miles across an area of country held by a battalion of the enemy whose resistance might delay their progress'. COHQ had also decided that, considering the time of the tides and the likely arrival of *Wehrmacht* reinforcements, the raid had to be completed within sixteen to twenty hours, or two tides.

It was largely considerations of time and armour that caused Mountbatten's instruction to plan an attack that enveloped Dieppe from the flanks to be modified to include the option of a frontal attack. The main reason was that the beach at Dieppe was considered to be the only landing point 'definitely viable for armour'. Sadly, this was based on an erroneous estimation of the consistency of the beach, and of the capabilities of the new Churchill tank, untried in combat, to climb the bank of large pebbles towards the Esplanade. The COHQ report described how the decision to take the frontal option was taken:

> 'On the 25 April, the first formal meeting to consider the plans for the operation... was held, with Vice-Admiral Mountbatten in the Chair. The question of a frontal assault was discussed... The Army representatives explained the reasons which led them to favour this form of assault. In the first place, to land any force as far west as Quiberville would make a surprise attack on Dieppe more difficult to achieve. In the second place, tanks landed on that beach would have to cross two rivers, which might prove to be considerable obstacles. In these circumstances, the bridges over them would have to be seized at a very early stage in order to make sure that they were not demolished by the enemy. Lastly, all available intelligence at that time showed that Dieppe was lightly held by a single low-category battalion...'

**Churchill Marks I to III were used by the Calgary Regiment at Dieppe. This example is a Mark III.**

Even though COHQ's had decided against the option of enveloping Dieppe from the flanks, the naval planners expressed doubt about the frontal assault, but not on naval grounds. Lieutenant General Montgomery, of South Eastern Command, argued strongly that the loss of surprise involved in the flank landings was a crucial factor

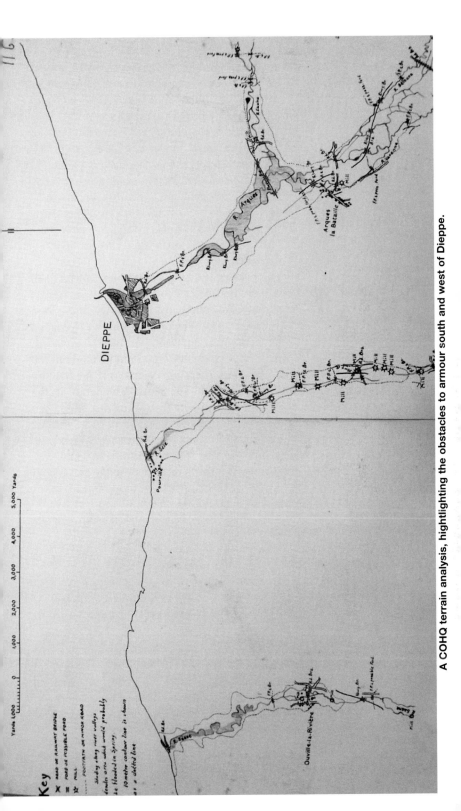

A COHQ terrain analysis, hightlighting the obstacles to armour south and west of Dieppe.

**Lieutenant General Montgomery photographed in the summer of 1942.**

in adopting the frontal assault against a town held by a few low-quality troops. However, as recorded in COHQ's report, the meeting was impressed by the assurance that:

*'The frontal assault would be preceded by a bombing attack on the town, to take place just before the craft carrying the assaulting troops touched down. This bombardment would be of maximum intensity, and it was thought that the defence would be too confused by it and by subsequent attacks from low-flying aircraft to be in a position to offer stout or prolonged resistance.'*

This section of the report concluded: 'The plan, which included the principal of a frontal assault preceded by bombing, was then adopted.' The Prime Minister was 'against indiscriminate bombing of French towns at night, but an exception would be made in the case of a coastal raid.' The mounting opposition of RAF Bomber Command was more serious: they saw their participation in the raids as an unwelcome and unprofitable distraction at a time when they were concentrating on mounting thousands of bomber raids on the German homeland. Also approved at the meeting was the Home Forces' nomination of 2nd Canadian Infantry Division, under Major General Robert's command, to provide the assault troops.

**Churchills practise coming ashore from a Tank Landing Craft. Note the engineers laying pailing across the shingle.**

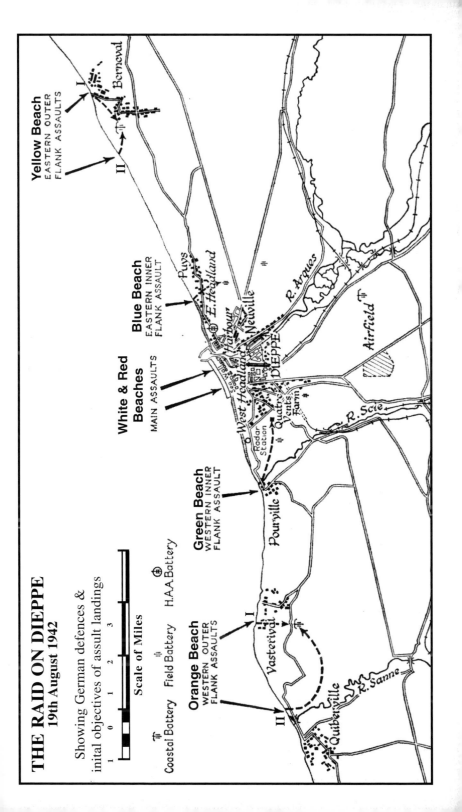

**THE RAID ON DIEPPE**
19th August 1942

Showing German defences &
inital objectives of assult landings

Scale of Miles

1    0    1    2    3

Coastal Battery  Field Battery  H.A.A.Battery

**Yellow Beach**
EASTERN OUTER
FLANK ASSAULTS

I
II

Berneval

**Blue Beach**
EASTERN INNER
FLANK ASSAULT

Puys
E.Headland

Harbour
Neuville

**White & Red Beaches**
MAIN ASSAULTS

West Headland  DIEPPE

Quatre
Vents
Farm

Radar
Station

R. Scie

R. Arques

Airfield

**Green Beach**
WESTERN INNER
FLANK ASSAULT

Pourville

**Orange Beach**
WESTERN OUTER
FLANK ASSAULTS

I
II

Vasterival

Quiberville

R. Sanne

Once the frontal attack plan had been approved, trials were conducted, on what were thought to be similar beaches, to confirm 'the performance of the Churchill tank on shingle.' The trials were successful, and the outline plan, responsibility for which had been delegated by COHQ and HQ Home Command to Lieutenant General Montgomery, was issued to the force command.

The framework of the plan was laid down by HQ South Eastern Command. However, General Roberts and his staff of Headquarters 2nd Canadian Division had to carry out a considerable amount of detailed planning and coordination between the various elements that made up the force, code named 'Simmerforce'. The force consisted of about 6,000 soldiers, of whom nearly 5,000 (two brigades) were Canadians, approximately 3,000 sailors crewing a total of 237 ships ranging from large to small, and almost seventy squadrons of aircraft. It should be noted that seven of the squadrons that eventually took part in the raid were from the US Army Air Force, while the US Army provided a detachment of fifty Rangers.

The outline of the plan that the Canadians worked on, at their HQ in Osborne House on the Isle of White, was as follows. Phase I was the embarkation of the force from the Isle of Wight and Solent ports; in Phase II, the Canadians would assault and occupy Dieppe; and in Phase III, the Engineers would carry out demolition tasks, and the intelligence officers would seize as many enemy documents as possible. Phase IV was the progressive withdrawal of the force and its re-embarkation, and in Phase V, the force would disembark on the southern coast and disperse to their camps in Sussex.

In the assault phase, 'Simmerforce' would attack the pair of *Wehrmacht* coastal batteries (code-named Hess and Goebels) on the cliffs approximately three and a half miles respectively to the east and west of Dieppe. They were to be destroyed by two companies from 1st Parachute Battalion in a preliminary attack. Once the batteries that dominated the approaches to Dieppe were destroyed, the main landings could take place. A mile and a half to the east and west, the rampart-like cliffs were broken by valleys leading down to the sea. At Puys (Blue Beach), a single battalion would land, while at the larger gap in the cliff at Pourville (Green Beach), two battalions would land in succession, with the second of the two battalions heading for its objective, the airfield at St Aubin. As already indicated, the main assault would be a frontal attack on Dieppe itself (Red and White Beaches), to be launched by two battalions in the first wave, supported by the Churchill tanks of the Calgary Regiment. Then the third battalion would land and push on to objectives inland, while a Royal Marine Commando would remain embarked as force reserve. The Royal Marines would also mount a cutting-out operation to seize German invasion barges in the port.

The list of missions grew to no fewer than nineteen separate objectives, and during the planning process there were attempts by other organisations to have their requirements incorporated into the raid, which was reported as becoming a 'serious nuisance.' For instance, the Air Ministry's Signals and Radio Direction Finding (RDF or Radar) Branch regarded the RDF station on the cliff a mile to the west of Dieppe as a 'target of opportunity'. Their interest is entirely understandable. The RDF station was in an area that was to be captured anyway by troops landing at Pourville, and it would be extremely useful, though not vital, for a technician to see what could be recovered. Unlike the vitally important Bruneval Raid, the Air Ministry was unwilling to risk sending a qualified scientist, which confirms the lower priority it attached to the raid. Once the RDF station was included in the growing list of objectives, an RAF radar technician who had volunteered for 'special operations' was extracted from a coastal radar site on the Devon coast. Flight Sergeant Nissenhall is referred to in orders and reports as 'the RDF Expert' and landed with the South Saskatchewan Regiment.

## The Canadians

Another factor in the planning of Dieppe was the increasing pressure 'to get the growing Canadian Force into action.' The Canadian Field Army had shrunk from a full Corps at the end of the Great War to a mere 4,500 regular troops, but Canada's military strength lay in its part-time militia units, which were quickly

**Canadians practice bayonet fighting during the long months of training. Note the bayonet scabbards are still on.**

**Ross Munro.**

mobilised and volunteered for service overseas. Meanwhile, volunteers swelled the number of recruits in training and, as in Britain, there were severe shortages of clothing and equipment. Despite these difficulties, the convoy carrying the 1st Canadian Division arrived in the Clyde on 17 December 1939, and from that date onwards they had trained and retrained. They were initially at Aldershot, which as described by Canadian Press reporter Ross Munro as 'not a good introduction to England'.

*'They will always recall Aldershot where every division went for its initial training overseas; grey, dull, uninspiring Aldershot, where they lived in big prison-like barracks, drilled on the huge squares and were inspected by royalty and brass. Aldershot is as stiff and forbidding as a drill sergeant major and in this oppressive barracks town the Canadians got their first impression of England. They did not like it much... The war seemed very unreal to them.'*

In the spring, and away from Aldershot to 'the stately homes and spacious estates requisitioned for camps and barracks,' the Canadians found that they were not to join the BEF in France as planned, but were to deploy to Norway. But before this move could take place, Norway was overrun and the Canadians returned to their camps in Southern England. When the Phoney War came to an end on 10 May 1940, as the Germans struck in the west, the Canadians were still in the UK. As the campaign disintegrated into defeat, there were proposals to reinforce the BEF in Calais, 'but it was obvious that Calais would not hold for long. It would be a useless waste of men to reinforce the Rifle Brigade, and the plan to use the Canadians was not put into force.' However, 1st Canadian Infantry Brigade sailed to Brest to join a British formation known as the 'Second BEF,' but this attempt to support the 'fading French Armies was doomed to failure'. Advancing to within forty miles of Paris, the Canadians received orders to withdraw as the French crumbled to defeat. The *Luftwaffe* harried 1st Canadian Brigade as it marched back to evacuation at Brest.

As the Battle of Britain was being fought, 2nd Canadian Infantry

Division (minus a brigade garrisoning strategically-important Iceland) arrived in Britain in August 1940. This division, and others that were to follow them across the Atlantic, initially took their place in defending the South Coast from the expected German invasion of the British Isles. Throughout the autumn of 1940 and into 1941, the Canadians shared the increasing privations of the British people, and became close to them, which resulted in many marriages, before the term 'GI bride' had even been invented.

As the threat of invasion gradually receded, and, like Napoleon, Hitler turned his attention to the east, the emphasis shifted to training. A year later, in the spring of 1942, the Canadians were champing at the bit, and wondering, with some justification, why they were not training back home in Canada. Officers censoring soldiers' letters home reported increasing resentment against their enforced inactivity. However, this 'trial for the patience of the Canadians' did mean that Canadian HQs and units were more comprehensively prepared than many of their British allies, whose formations were constantly being called on to provide battle-casualty replacements for the Mediterranean and Far East theatres.

In the spring of 1942, the people of Horsham in Sussex became aware that the 2nd Canadian Division's camps surrounding their town were empty. They were used to the Canadians disappearing on exercise, but not for so long. The 2nd Division had moved to the

**A Canadian crewed Churchill batters down an obstacle in one of the urban training areas in early 1942.**

Above: Canadian infantry train in the 'blitzed' ruins of an English town

Left: Major General 'Ham' Roberts, Officer Commander 2nd Canadian Division.

Below: A Mark I Churchill desembarking from a Tank Landing Craft on the Isle of Wight.

T.L.C. 303.

Isle of Wight, where with the Solent between it and the mainland, they were to train in great secrecy for the Dieppe raid. However, with the RAF yet to establish supremacy of the skies above the Isle of Wight, the *Luftwaffe* noted the growing number of vessels of all types assembling in the small ports along the Solent.

The training objective was simple: to prepare for the raid. However, as mentioned earlier, COHQ's report records that there were no fewer than nineteen enabling objectives. These objectives, all with a strong commando flavour, ranged from 'General agility training particularly up steep places of almost cliff gradient' through 'Practice with the actual loads which it was proposed would be carried by the assaulting troops' to, 'Street fighting with particular reference to intercommunication between small interdependent detachments'. This latter training took place amongst 'blitzed buildings of West Cowes and Yarmouth, which daily rang to the sound of small arms and the crack of exploding grenades'. Amphibious training with landing craft, especially when the Calgary Regiment and their new 40-ton Churchill tanks began practising loading and off-loading with the new Landing Craft Tank (LCT), produced considerable speculation. However, only a handful of officers at Major General Robert's Headquarters knew the reason behind this rigorous commando-type training.

A couple of exerpts from war diaries give a flavour of the Canadians' training. On 8 June 1942, the adjutant of the South Saskatchewan Regiment recorded the day's activities for the battalion:

> 'HQ Coy on wire cutting, map and compass work. A Coy crossing wire obstacles, climbing and swimming. B Coy assault work and compass march. C Coy unarmed combat. Route march. D Coy route march and lecture on grenades. All coys on night schemes, compass march or crossing wire obstacles. Returning to camp at 0100 hours where they received a hot drink.'

Sleep was a precious commodity, and the South Saskatchewans were out early the next day, with reveille sounded at 0500 hours. The following day's programme included amphibious training with LCAs. The soldiers of the Calgary Regiment had a seemingly easier physical regime, but after training, they had to spend many sleep-depriving hours maintaining their Churchill tanks. Their war diary described a typical day during their preparations.

> '23 May 42: 0600 hrs – Embarking, craft afloat.
> 0630 hrs to 0830 hrs – Cruise.

**A Mark I Churchill climbing a seawall via a 'lumber ramp' during training.**

*0830 hrs to 0900 hrs – Disembarking exercise. Craft afloat and withdrawn when unloaded.*
*1000 hrs to 1300 hrs – Gunnery and small arms training.*
*1430 hrs to 1800 hrs –Troop Training.'*

The Dieppe Raid was to be the first amphibious attack in which armour was to be used. So the Calgary Regiment were not only training, they were also taking on an element of development work. This included perfecting the waterproofing of the Churchills, which now sported the characteristic extensions to their exhaust pipes.

Sergeant Major Dumais of the Fusiliers Mont Royal has written an account of the training from a soldier's point of view:

*'Our training as commandos was designed to transform us from hard and well disciplined troops into men who refused to give up. Physical and psychological resistance had to be brought to a peak. To this end, we drove our men more and more ruthlessly... Our assault courses went uphill, naturally; but we made them go over it five or six times until they could not stand up... We trained in most dangerous conditions, climbing vertical cliffs in the minimum time, and crossed rivers on a rope... Each man had to get over with his full equipment... We lived in the open for several weeks with only a ground-sheet, a gas-cape, and two blankets for protection. We slept in our damp uniforms and when it rained we got wetter.*

*'There was no question of using blanks for training: when firing around or over our troops, we used regular service ammunition. Bullets were one thing – they tend to go where they are aimed – but grenades, mortar bombs and shells are quite another... I was coming out of a building that we used for house-to-house fighting. I heard "Take cover!" and dived for the ground – but never got there. I was lifted, spun around, and woke up with my head in the corner, stunned and at first deaf but without a scratch.'*

The Royal Canadian Engineers trained particularly hard with both the tanks and infantry, but their most important task was to open routes across the beaches, which in the case of Dieppe was up onto the open Esplanade. This involved getting the tanks over the six-foot-high seawall, emphasised in intelligence photographs and information as the most serious obstacle. Captain Whitaker wrote:

*'For the high walls, the sappers devised wooden ramps or stairways for the tanks to climb. Each of these ramps was made of five tons of lumber. A squad of 30 men trained hard to carry these loads an anticipated 30 yards and then assemble the ramps in an incredible five minutes.'*

After a month's intensive training, General Roberts noted a steady improvement in the time in which speed marches were completed, better shooting results and favourable comment on tact-ical exercises, COHQ reported:

*'By the 13th June, the troops were deemed to be sufficiently*

**The Calgary muster with 'crews front' before embarking for Exercise Yukon II.**

Canadian soldiers being briefed on their part in Operation Rutter.

trained, and a full-scale exercise was carried out. It took place near Bridport on a coast as nearly as possible resembling that which was to be assaulted. The exercise was given the code name "Yukon I" ...It was not altogether successful and revealed certain deficiencies in the training of all three services. The main errors were, that a landing was made on the wrong beach, that many of the Tank Landing Craft were late, that some of the landings took place at the wrong time and in broad daylight, that the liaison between personnel of the Royal Engineers and the Infantry was defective and that the infantry progressed inland at a very slow rate.

'Not altogether successful' was not how the Canadians viewed the assault exercise on the Dorset coast at Bridport. It was a disaster. Battalions were landed up to two miles from their designated beaches, and, as in the case of the Calgary Regiment, some units landed well behind schedule. A HQ South Eastern Command officer reported that as a result of the appalling landing:

'The division fell into an indescribable confusion, which was in itself sufficient to throw doubt on the feasibility of the operation, even though there was no enemy present to turn confusion into bloodshed and slaughter.'

Without a successful rehearsal, Admiral Mountbatten could not authorise Operation Rutter to proceed. As explained in his HQ's post-operational review:

'On receiving a report of this exercise, the Chief of Combined Operations decided to hold a second exercise known as "Yukon II" on the 23rd June. This decision was not reached without some difficulty, for to carry it out entailed a postponement of the operation. The Chief of Combined Operations, however, considered it essential for another exercise to take place, and the postponement was accepted. This second exercise, which was witnessed by the Chief of Combined Operations, was much more successful and he therefore decided to carry out the operation at the first favourable

30

*date after the 24th June.'*

Though still far from prefect (particularly in naval aspects), there was sufficient improvement and assurances of lessons being learned to allow Operation Rutter to proceed. The troops were embarked, briefed, and sealed from contact with those not taking part in the operation.

Only on 27 June were the majority of the officers made aware of the fact that they were training for an actual operation rather than an exercise; the men were only briefed on 2 July when they embarked on their landing ships and craft. Unaware that the Rutter plan was already unravelling, the soldiers were pleased at the prospect of action. Captain Denis Whitaker wrote of the Canadians' optimism:

**Canadian officers photographed during Yukon I**

> *'We had trained hard; we were confident that we were ready for action – as fit and tough and skilled as a soldier could be. We infantrymen saw ourselves surging onto the beach under the umbrella of thundering naval guns.'*

## Cancellation

While the Force waited in its ships and landing craft all assembled in the Isle of Wight's Solent ports, 'during the last week in June and the first week in July, the weather intervened.' This was a sustained period of poor weather, with winds well above Force 3, a sea state that for much of the period precluded amphibious operations with tanks, and placed the vital airborne element of the plan out of the question. 'The weather continued to be unsuitable and on the 5 July, the operation was postponed.' The delay led to another modification of Rutter's plan:

> *'It had been worked out that, if the expedition was to take place on the 7th July, it would be impossible, owing to the state of the tide, to re-embark the tanks until some three hours later than would have been the case on Saturday, the 4th July, and that, in consequence, three hours further air cover would be necessary. The Military Force Commander now expressed the opinion that these extra hours would give the enemy an opportunity to organise infantry and artillery opposition on a scale which might prejudice the re-embarkation. The Force Commanders, therefore, agreed... that in their view the operation should not be carried out in its original*

*form on the 7th July, and that the plan had a diminishing chance of success as each day passed. The Chief of Combined Operations thereupon directed the Force Commanders to consider a modified plan whereby the operation should take place on one tide. It would begin as nearly as possible to the time of low-water and be completed or nearly completed by the next following high-water.'*

This 'one-tide' plan enabled the RAF air support to be increased, as the duration of the operation would be reduced from twenty hours to just twelve hours. With the tanks needing to withdraw before the tide receded too far, the time they would be ashore would be reduced. Consequently, tasks such as the attack on the St Aubin aerodrome and on the German divisional headquarters at Arques-la-Bataille would be without tank support. It would also not be possible to carry out a full intelligence search of these facilities, and there was only time to make a few quick demolitions. 'This plan commended itself to the Force Commanders and it was agreed to adopt it.'

But on 7 July, before the abbreviated plan could come into effect and the Canadians go ashore at Dieppe, the enemy intervened. The Combined Ops report recorded that:

*'While awaiting the order to proceed against the enemy,... some of the force was anchored in Yarmouth Roads, some in Cowes Roads and the remainder in Southampton Water... at 0615 hours four German fighter bombers, believed to be FW 190s, dropped four 500 kilogram bombs on HMS* Princess Astrid *and HMS* Princess Josephine Charlotte *lying in Yarmouth Roads with troops on board. Both ships were hit and the damage done to HMS* Princess Josephine Charlotte *was severe. The bomb went through the mess decks into the engine room, thence through the bottom of the ship and exploded underneath; putting the ship out of commission ... Whether the enemy had an inkling that the expedition was about to sail cannot be known for certain. He made frequent air reconnaissance flights during the last week of June and the first week of July.'*

The weather continued to be bad, and with two ships now out of action, the operation was formally cancelled on 7 July.

The force of some 10,000 men returned from the Isle of Wight to their normal bases around the country. Obviously, all these fully-briefed naval personnel and troops knew about the operation in considerable detail. The official report commented that, 'There is no doubt that talk and rumours were rife for some time after the dispersal of the Force'. The possibility of there having been a leak concerning the operation, and that it was picked up and reported by enemy agents, was investigated at the time. The likelihood of this having occured has been hotly debated ever since. However, at the time it was assessed that enemy intelligence reports would have indicated that this was a cancelled raid, not one that was about to happen.

## Revival of the Operation

The Rutter plan had been shelved, but, there were still hopes to revive the operation. The process by which the raid was revived just six weeks later is still shrouded with secrecy and has developed its own mythology. Suffice it to say that, as recorded by Captain Whitaker, there was a feeling that the operation 'was being pushed relentlessly towards its conclusion by a powerful unseen force'.

Reasons behind this unseen force have been hotly debated. Mountbatten perhaps provided a clue when he wrote:

> 'Since we cannot conceal from the Germans that we are intending operations, and, indeed, part of the object of these operations is to keep them in a state of suspense, I welcome any publicity that might arise from this scheme.'

This clearly indicates the intent to keep German divisions in the West. It is also reported that the American reaction to the cancellation of Rutter was a restatement of their threat: if the British did not take action, they would reconsider the 'Germany-first'

**Focke Wulf 190. German aircraft were still able to range across Southern Britain and attack opportunity targets in early 1942.**

decision and concentrate on the Pacific theatre. Consequently, on 27 July, the Chiefs of Staff Committee issued a new Directive to Admiral Mountbatten. The COHQ report records that:

> 'The next most favourable period for carrying out a raid on Dieppe would occur during August. It was accordingly decided to re-mount the operation, the code name for which was changed from "Rutter" to "Jubilee".'

The basic plan remained similar, but with the obvious change of substituting commandos for paratroopers for the attack on the flanking coastal batteries. Mountbatten's report goes on to explain why:

> 'It was decided that the attacks on the extreme flanks, to capture

**Commandos with their distinctive 'cap comforters' taking part in boat training in Scotland.**

*the batteries at Berneval on the east and Varengeville on the west of*
*Dieppe, should be made not by airborne troops but by commandos*
*of the Special Service Brigade. The chief reason for this change was*
*that, though the weather might be suitable for the Naval passage*
*and for the landing of infantry and tanks and their re-embarkation,*
*it might not be possible to use airborne troops, who have to depend*
*for success on conditions different from those of a Naval operation.*
*. . In point of fact, on the day of the operation, the weather*
*conditions, though satisfactory from the Naval point of view, would*
*have made the employment of airborne troops impossible. . . In fact,*
*had airborne troops not been excluded, the operation would not have*
*taken place.'*

In the revised Jubilee plan there were, however, other crucial but
less obvious changes. These included some elements of the original

Rutter plan on which the entire raid had
been predicated. The most important
change was that of air support. The Navy
had turned down Mountbatten's request
for naval gunfire support from capital
ships: 'Battleships in the Channel! Are
you mad, Dickey?' Thus with only eight
Hunt Class destroyers in close support,
each mounting four or six of the smallest
naval gun; the four-inch firing only a
thirty-six pound shell, the plan relied on
the effect of an intense air bombardment
with 150 bomber sorties striking the town
and the headlands to the east and west of
Dieppe. However, during the planning
process the 'overpowering' bombing raid
was cancelled. Various reasons have been
advanced, including political dislike of
bombing a French town, Bomber
Command's reluctance to be diverted
from its offensive against Germany, and
the fact that the bombing would not have
been 'overwhelming,' as a high-level
attack would have been too inaccurate to
be effective. Conversely, it was also
suggested that bombing would create too
much rubble in the streets, and finally,

**An RAF Boston medium bomber flying during Operation Jubilee.**

that the preliminary raid may have alerted the enemy. In the event, the vast majority of the sorties mounted by the air forces were by fighters and fighter-bombers, with only sixty-two being launched by medium bombers. Despite the lack of bomber support, the arguable need for additional naval gunfire support does not appear to have been reviewed.

In great secrecy, Operation Jubilee was prepared. The troops had completed the necessary training and were already familiar with their tasks and, therefore, final preparations would be minimal. It will be remembered that the troops detailed to take part in Operation Rutter had been kept sealed on board the landing craft

**RAF ground crew prepare bombs for the Dieppe Raid.**

for five days before its cancellation, but according to COHQ:

> 'It was decided when the operation was remounted as "Jubilee" that the troops should be kept in ignorance of what was required of them until the last moment and not be briefed until a few hours before sailing.'

## The US Rangers

Before concluding, it is worth expanding on the presence of the US Rangers amongst the Jubilee Assault Force. In the *Official History Grand Strategy* series, in the meeting of 9 June 1942:

> 'Mr Roosevelt, he said, had stressed the great need for American soldiers to be given the opportunity of fighting (in the west) as soon as possible.'

An American Brigadier General attached to COHQ readily agreed, and provided fifty members of 1st US Rangers, who had been raised from among the first US units to cross the Atlantic, thus reviving a great American military tradition. The volunteers had been trained at the Commando Training Centre alongside Royal Marine and Army commandos at Achnacarry House in the Highlands of Scotland, and were consequently familiar with British and Canadian methods. The four officers and forty-six men were to be allocated in small groups across the raiding force. Other groups of American officers were present as observers, mainly at the various HQs.

**President Roosevelt.**

On 18 August 1942, the force, with all its component parts of various nations representing Combined Operations, and all three Services, was assembling. By the following day, the force was reported ready, and final authorisation was given. Briefings were underway and Operation Jubilee was set to go.

# Chapter Two

# THE DEFENDERS OF DIEPPE

At the very outset of planning the raid, two of the vital prerequisites that were agreed were that Dieppe could only be attacked if it were lightly held by the enemy, and that the raiders would achieve 'total surprise.' Despite repeated assurances by the Headquarters of Combined Ops, Home Command and the Canadian Forces, neither of these prerequisites was to be met on the beaches of Dieppe.

The Germans had arrived on the northern coast of France in the last days of May 1940. Their focus had initially been on preparing for the invasion of Britain (Operation Sea Lion), but latterly they had increasingly concentrated on defence of the coastline. British intelligence assumed that it was 110th Division that was playing this defensive role in the Dieppe area, with its Headquarters at Arques-la-Bataille on the south-western outskirts of Dieppe. Details of an Operation Rutter intelligence briefing held on 25 April 1942 were recorded in the COHQ report:

> 'all available intelligence at that time showed that Dieppe was lightly held by a single low-category battalion supported by ten AA guns, three or four light anti-aircraft guns, one four-gun dual-purpose battery and four coast defence batteries. Furthermore, the troops in Dieppe, numbering, it was thought, not more than 1,400 all told, could not be heavily reinforced for some time. After five hours the total number of reinforcements which could reach them would not, it was considered, exceed 2,500 men; only from the eighth hour of the attack onwards might important reserves begin to arrive, mainly from Rouen and from the east. Thus, at the end of fifteen hours, the maximum number of enemy troops which might, in the most favourable circumstances, be brought into action, would be in the neighbourhood of 6,500 men.'

Much of the intelligence was, however, incorrect: for example, in the summer of 1942, 110th Division was fighting on the Eastern Front. The division at Dieppe was in fact 302nd Infantry Division, which had been raised during the autumn of 1940 in Bavaria as a low-category formation. *Hauptman* Lindener, staff adjutant of 571 *Infanterie* Regiment commented on the quality of the division, 'The

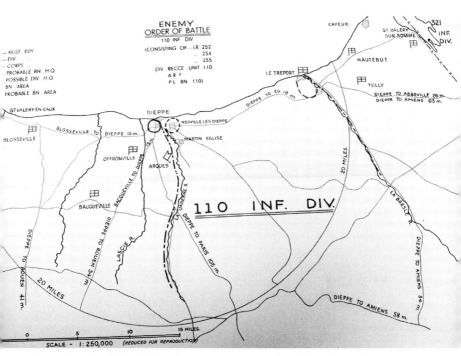

**A map showing the Allied intelligence assessment in early 1942, which proved to be incorrect in most detail.**

coastal-defence divisions were second class. This is a hard word but essentially true.' Not only were men of a low physical grade being called up, but men from the newly-captured territories that had been annexed into Germany were already being conscripted into the *Wehrmacht*. The 6,000 soldiers of 302nd moved to France in April 1941 with a slim establishment and little equipment, particularly vehicles. After a year, *Generalmajor* Conrad Haase moved his headquarters from Arques-la-Bataille to Envermeu, some seven miles from Dieppe. This was at about the same time Allied intelligence was assembling information on potential targets. Not only did intelligence identify the wrong division and an incorrect HQ location, but they also failed to identify the Germans' true strength in Dieppe, which was greater than anticipated. The cumulative effect of these and other errors led to Admiral Mountbatten's comment that 'the intelligence was woefully inadequate.'

Across the Channel, events such as the Bruneval and St Nazaire raids earlier in the year had prompted the Germans to strengthen their coastal defences. In addition, as his campaign in Russia prospered, Hitler realised that the Allies were bound to take some action in the west to help relieve the pressure on the Red Army. If he was in any doubt, the political necessity of Allied action in the west was confirmed by reports of Molotov's visit to London in May 1942, and by the widely reported pressure for 'A Second Front Now' (Operation Sledgehammer). The Führer concluded that he needed to reinforce the west. In March 1942, he issued Führer Order Number Forty. The important section read:

'The coastline of Europe will, in the coming months, be subject to the danger of enemy landings in force... Even enemy landings with limited objectives can seriously interfere

**Adolf Hitler – Political and *de facto* military leader of the Third Reich.**

with our own plans if they result in the enemy gaining a toehold on the coast... Enemy forces that have landed must be destroyed or thrown back into the sea by immediate counter attack.'

Allied intelligence failed to identify the resulting moves of units and formations in the late spring and summer of 1942. As Rutter gave way to Jubilee, there was little demand for up-to-date intelligence, and such information that was available, unlike that supplied for D-Day, was rarely detailed below battalion level.

*Feldmarschall* **von Rundstedt**

During the early spring, Commander-in-Chief West *Feldmarshall* von Rundstedt saw his strength in combat formations gradually growing until he had thirty-six divisions under command, most of which were concentrated along the Dutch, Belgian and the French coastlines. The new arrivals were nearly all infantry divisions, but they were supported by a number of panzer and SS divisions. The problem was that these reinforcements were either low-category, such as 302nd at Dieppe, or had returned from the

The defences overprint map issued to the raiding force for intelligence briefing. It was mainly based on air photography.

The Dieppe Esplanada: Alli intelligence rel heavily on pre-war picture postcards of Dieppe for briefing the raiders.

Eastern Front as little more than a cadre, to be built up and retrained. As the pace of the campaign in Russia increased, there were continuous demands on formations in the west to provide drafts of battle-casualty replacements. It was no surprise to von Rundstedt that Hitler's OKH inspecting officers found that, by summer 1942, many of the units manning defences in the Dieppe area were under strength, and often missing whole companies from their order of battle. However, as Hitler became increasingly aware of the threat to the Channel and Atlantic coasts, under-manning started to be addressed, especially as the *Luftwaffe* had noticed a marked increase in shipping in the south coast ports. Air photography sorties provided confirmation of an increase in small naval ships and landing craft, from 1,146 on 3 June 1942 to a total of 2,802 on 23 July. The Germans were not, however, totally convinced, as it is recorded that they were 'struck above all by the apparent neglect of any attempt at camouflage or concealment, suggesting a double bluff or deception.' However, German Army staff officers erroneously calculated, from the air photography information, that the British could land 300,000 men on the northern coast of France between the Pas de Calais and Normandy in just three days. Consequently, Hitler continued to reinforce the west and put his forces on state of high alert, reinforced by a series of directives and special orders to commanders and the soldiers defending the coastline.

While troops were disengaged and transported from the Russian Front, von Rundstedt and his staff tried to identify the target for what they correctly assessed would be an operational-level raid rather than a full invasion. Options included the U-boat bases on the western coast, the Brittany Peninsular, or 'an attack to capture a strong point or to disrupt air or naval operations for some time.' The lack of a unified intelligence system, and the tendency of the German Services and special interest factions to talk up intelligence to their own ends, prevented a coherent picture of Allied intentions from being developed. This was to be a consistent factor in the west, which the Allies increasingly exploited to their own purposes through the Bletchley Park code breaker's descriptions of German signal traffic and double agents.

### The Defences of Dieppe

In 1942, Allied intelligence lacked the detailed information that it subsequently developed in the period before D-Day. Much of the detail listed below was therefore unknown to Allied operational planners, but it is important to include it here if we are to make sense of the German reaction to the raid.

302nd Division had its right or eastern boundary on the River Somme at Abbeville, and held fifty miles of coast west to a point about ten miles beyond Dieppe. In practice, this was not the impossible task that it seemed, because much of the coastline was high chalk cliffs, with only a few ways up onto the farmland beyond. This allowed the Germans to concentrate their forces at important locations along the coast and at key points such as Fortress or '*Festung* Dieppe,' which they expected, at this stage of the war, to be subject to a large raid rather than an invasion. The German report after Dieppe specifically noted that their tactics were not to defend every defile through the cliffs and every beach, but just those near an objective that could be used by an enemy raiding party.

The Todt Organisation had, with the aid of slave labour drafted from every corner of occupied Europe, started in the autumn of 1941 to construct *Festung* Dieppe. The town and most of its defences were surrounded by a high barbed wire fence made up of several roles of concertina wire along its length. Along the sea front, reinforced concrete pillboxes, gun casemates, shelter bunkers, and strong points, some built into existing buildings, were beginning to replace field fortifications. Meanwhile, on the two headlands, gun positions dominating the beach below were tunnelled out of the chalk. For the Allies, construction of pillboxes was easily picked up on vertical air photographs, but the enhancements to and use of the existing tunnels in the cliffs below the headlands were missed.

However, the existence of tunnels in the cliffs was known to generations of British ferry visitors to Dieppe. Churchill himself recounted how:

> 'One night when I was talking about this business beforehand to Mrs Churchill [who had lived for several years in Dieppe in the Twenties], *she spoke about those caves and said what a help they would be to the enemy. I have seen them myself when landing at Dieppe. The whole cliff is pockmarked.'*

RAF air photograph interpreters using a stereoscope.

The presence of guns in the mouths of caves in the cliff might well have been revealed by sufficiently oblique air-photography sorties, but few were authorised, and little information on the cliffs was gained. Although great strides had been made in developing photo-reconnaissance, there were still insufficient RAF air-photo interpreters, and skill levels were still developing but were still well short of the standards reached by 1944. Even so, lack of information on the cliffs was a significant failure, and many veterans believe that the presence of German observation officers, guns and machine guns positioned in the caves did the most to halt the frontal attack on Dieppe. However, it should be noted that the Germans had mounted their guns so that they could be drawn back into the cliff to avoid both observation and enemy fire, and it is reasonable to assume that new embrasures in the chalk were well camouflaged.

The COHQ report records that holding the immediate Dieppe

Photographed after the battle a German gun crew pose by their 75mm in the mouth of a cave in the Western Headland.

M.G. AND LIGHT GUN EMPLACEMENTS

An air photograph used for briefing, showing the 'cave' positions dug into the Eastern Headland overlooking the entrance to the Avant Port.

area was *Oberstleutnant* Hermann Bartelt's 571 *Infanterie* Regiment:

> '. . .with two battalions forward and one in reserve, to a depth of about seven miles. In general, the defences were sited in an anti-raid role as opposed to an anti-invasion role, and the greater part of the available firepower was concentrated to cover the landing beaches. The II Battalion, holding the town itself, west of the river, occupied a position of about 1,500 yards deep, and the landward defences were sited to deal only with an attack from the rear by paratroops.'

Bartelt's forward or tactical headquarters was located in some newly built concrete bunkers on the hillside to the west of the town. From here he could look out across the seaward approaches to Dieppe and downward to Red and White Beaches and the Esplanade.

It has been consistently suggested that with general concern about a raid, Bartelt redeployed his forces in Dieppe, first increasing the defenders to two battalions on 10 July, and then to all three of his battalions in early August 1942. This allegedly brought the number of troops in the town to 3,500. This is incorrect, as it is now apparent that there was a single battalion of infantry in Dieppe. However, there were supporting troops, particularly *Kriegsmarine* gunners and *Luftwaffe* anti-tank gunners who may have been reinforced to a certain extent. The reinforcement that was made by *Oberstleutnant* Bartelt was to move the centre of gravity of his flanking battalions closer to Dieppe, which thinned the defences along the rugged coastline to the east and west.

Defensive preparations around Dieppe had been considerable, and the amount of concrete used in their construction, though nothing like as heavy as port defences were to become over the following two years, still gave the coastal infantry garrison a significant advantage. Post-operational intelligence described the pillboxes that the Canadians encountered along the seafront:

> 'One pillbox containing machine guns was built of concrete about 6 ft 6 ins high, with only 4ft showing above the ground. The walls and the roof were about 1½ ft thick, and the door was about 2 ft thick. This pillbox was circular with an internal diameter of 10 ft, and only had one horizontal fire slit. Another pillbox, which contained a 4.7cm anti-tank gun, was of a similar construction but square instead of round. The roof and walls were estimated to be 3 ft thick.'

In addition, concrete walls '8 ft high and 3-4 ft thick' had been built across most of the roads from the Esplanade into the town. The few exits that remained only had easily-blocked gaps in the walls for light vehicles about eight feet wide. All of these obstacles were found to be covered with machine gun and anti-tank fire.

Surrounding *Festung* Dieppe were no fewer than four major artillery batteries, mainly using captured French guns, which were either tasked to take on enemy shipping or were designed to engage a landing force, either on the beaches or on the landward approaches to the town. Two of these, as already mentioned, were flanking batteries located on the cliffs at Berneval and Varengeville, which are covered in detail at Chapters 4 and 5. A battery located near Arques-la-Bataille, inland from the town, housed four 150mm guns, which could engage targets virtually anywhere in the raid's area, provided of course that there was an observer to give fire-direction orders. A fourth battery (four 150mm guns) was located at Mesnil-Val, west of le Treport, that was sited to provide the Berneval area with mutual support. The fire of these large-calibre guns was supplemented by smaller pieces, many of which were also captured and were mostly located within Dieppe's barbed-wire perimeter. In addition, four lesser batteries, each of four 100mm guns, were deployed to the west and to the east of Dieppe, while covering the seafront were eight of the renowned but now obsolescent French 75mm guns. This gives a total of forty-five artillery pieces of various calibres, to which must be added the forty-five 81mm medium mortars of a coastal infantry regiment. This artillery total was certainly not consistent with the COHQ definition of 'lightly held.'

Other guns marked on the overprinted maps were the *Wehrmacht* and *Luftwaffe* anti-aircraft guns defending the town and

Sandbag emplacements were still common place. This position was on the Dieppe Esplanade overlooking Red and White beaches.

A newly built and well camouflaged casemate on the coast near Dieppe.

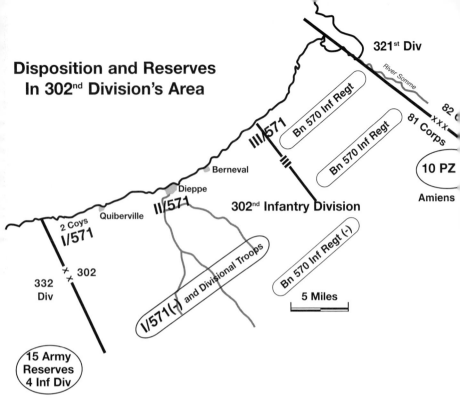

## Disposition and Reserves In 302nd Division's Area

321st Div

River Somme

82

xxx

81 Corps

Bn 570 Inf Regt

Bn 570 Inf Regt

III/571

10 PZ

Amiens

Berneval

Dieppe

II/571

302nd Infantry Division

Quiberville

2 Coys

I/571

Bn 570 Inf Regt (-)

I/571(-) and Divisional Troops

x x 302

332 Div

5 Miles

15 Army Reserves 4 Inf Div

the St Aubin airfield. These were various calibres, from the light 20mm to the heavy 88mm. Again, the volume of fire that would face the Allied air forces' fighter-bombers was under-estimated. *Kriegsmarine* gunners and some marines manned defensive positions in the immediate area of the port.

571 *Infanterie* Regiment's local reserve was provided by a part of its 1st infantry battalion, which was probably located at Bacqueville (over eleven miles from Dieppe), ready to deploy wherever it was required on the regimental front. For mobility, the Germans had some troop-carrying transport, but much of the immediate reserve relied on marching or bicycle, as the regiment was generally short of transport.

Further away, General Kuntzen's *LXXXI Korps's* reserve of four infantry battalions, with some transport, was located thirty-five miles to the south-west of Dieppe, though it was unlikely that they could have concentrated significant combat power within eight hours. The final German reserve was 10th Panzer Division, which intelligence reported in early July to be occupying barracks in the area of Amiens, which was also only eight hours' march away. Clearly, the landing force would be unable to deal with panzers,

The picture postcard seaside resort village Pourville was held by a platoon from 8 *Kompanie,* 571 *Infantarie* Regiment.

A twin MG 34 anti-aircraft mount in a coastal field position photographed in early 1942.

and their presence within striking distance of Dieppe is one of the factors that led to the raid being confined to a single tide. The withdrawal and re-embarkation was to start at 1100, six hours after the landing, which was a significant reduction from the fifteen hours ashore envisaged in the original Rutter plan.

Outside *Festung* Dieppe, all along the coast, gullies leading up from the beach were choked with rolls of concertina wire, laced with mines and shells triggered by trip wires. Across the few small beaches to east and west of Dieppe, anti-tank walls were built, and most of the gullies were covered by patrols; even battalion-sized beaches such as Pourville (Green Beach) had a permanent garrison of little more than a platoon (forty to fifty men). In this case, they were from 8 *Kompanie* 571 *Infanterie* Regiment, with the remainder of the company holding the Eastern Headland.

The Allies were still working on the April intelligence that predated Hitler's change of heart on the defences of Dieppe and the other Channel ports. Lieutenant Colonel Lord Lovat, commanding 4 Commando wondered,

> '*Did Ham Roberts know what he was up against before starting? I suggest the answer is no.* [Lt Col] *Merritt confirms that, prior to departure for the operation, he knew little about the Germans, or how their Commander was likely to react.*'

'Don't worry,' the General Roberts said during his briefing at HQ 2nd Canadian Division, 'it will be a piece of cake.'

### State of Alert

On 20 July, *Oberstgeneral* Curt Haase issued Fifteenth Army orders activating 'the highest degree of watchfulness and readiness for action' for three periods of what were assessed to be favourable tide and moon. They were 27 July to 3 August, 10 to 19 August, and 25 August to 1 September. This state of readiness required 'all personnel to sleep fully clothed at or near their posts.' This order was supplemented by an exhortation to his soldiers to 'Be on guard! Eyes and ears alert! Kick the Anglo-American and his helpers in the snout'. On 10 August, as the latest period of high alert began, a special order of the day was issued. *Oberstgeneral* Haase again warned of an impending landing, and went on to describe the threat that *LXXXI Korps* faced:

> '*The information in our hands makes it clear that the Anglo-Americans will be forced, in spite of themselves, by the wretched predicament of the Russians to undertake some operations in the*

**The German defenders were regularly exercised and were able to respond quickly to any landing**

*West in the near future.*

*Soldiers, you must realise that it will be a very sticky business! Bombs and naval guns, sea weapons and commandos, assault craft and parachutists, airborne troops and hostile citizens, sabotage and murder will have to be coped with. Steady nerves will be required if we are not to go under.*

*Fear does not exist! When the hail of fire pours down upon you, you must wipe your eyes and ears, clutch your weapons harder and defend yourselves as never before!*

*THEM or US! That must be our watchword!*

*The German Army has in the past received all kinds of tasks from the Führer and has always carried them out. The Army will carry out this task too. My soldiers, you won't fail! I have looked into your eyes! You are German men!*

*You will willingly and bravely do your duty!*

*Do this and you will remain victorious!*

*Long live our people and our Fatherland!*
*Long live our Führer Adolf Hitler!'*

In response to Commander Fifteenth Army's exhortations to fight to the last, *Generalmajor* Haase required all of his officers to parade at divisional headquarters to formally swear an oath to hold their position to death. With the oaths taken, Haase himself dramatically swore that he 'would rather die than retreat or surrender'. Despite exhortations and oaths, *Hauptman* Lindner explained that, without a visible threat, it was difficult to maintain a high state of alert.

> *'It was very quiet, day after day nothing. We had difficulty with the sentries guarding the coast; the poor man walking with his rifle along the cliffs. Nothing happened but the waves coming and going. Sometimes they slept. Yes, we had a problem keeping them awake.'*

No doubt mindful of the need not to keep his troops on a high state of alert for longer than was strictly necessary, and the decreasing return from doing so, Commander Fifteenth Army reduced the state of readiness on 18 August. However, *Generalmajor* Haase decided that 302nd *Infanterie* Division would remain on Red Alert for another night before standing down after dawn on the fateful day of 19 August 1942. His divisional order read

> *'The night 18/19th can be regarded as suitable for enemy raiding operations. Commanders of coastal defences are to maintain troops at the Threatened Danger Alert.'*

**Life for the German defenders of France's northern coast was far from uncomfortable but dull. These soldiers relax on the terrace of the Old Château, Dieppe.**

# CHAPTER THREE

# EMBARKATION AND ENCOUNTER AT SEA

The decision to launch the raid was kept from 2nd Canadian Division and the rest of the raiding force until the last moment. On 10 August, the Calgary Regiment were required to waterproof their Churchill tanks in preparation for what they were told was yet another Combined Operations demonstration. Meanwhile, General Robert's staff issued orders for his soldiers to prepare for Exercise Ford I, II and III; a series of innocent-sounding convoy exercises, starting on 15 August 1942.

Measures to maintain security and to keep the land component of the force from speculating about what was going on were comprehensive. COHQ records that 'One battalion arrived to take part... with empty ammunition boxes, being under the impression that it was to take part in yet another exercise and being anxious to save weight.' Their real ammunition, stacked on the quay side, was handed over to a puzzled quartermaster on arrival at the port.

The first occasion that any one at unit level knew of the raid's revival was when Major General Roberts summoned all senior battalion HQ officers to an equally innocent-sounding lecture at a village near Chichester. The Jubilee plan was essentially the same as that for Operation Rutter, including some changes already made, such as the restriction to one tide, and replacing airborne troops with two Army commando units. There was also a new chain of command: Lieutenant General Montgomery, to whom much of the detailed planning had been delegated, was promoted to command the Eighth Army in Egypt. Now the chain of command led from Admiral Mountbatten to Canadian Generals McNaughton, Crerar and Roberts, who, under huge political, national and military pressure, had little choice but to agree to go ahead with the plan.

**The early version of 2nd Canadian Division's badge featured a yellow 'C II' woven on a blue background**

Major Glenn of the Calgary Regiment was in a staff car following the tank transporters taking his Churchills to Gosport for the 'demonstration' when,

> 'All of a sudden, the bloody column comes to a halt and we are called to a conference in a little air-raid shelter by the side of the road, no lights or anything. We were shown some aerial photographs, taken that afternoon over Dieppe. It was on again...'

Especially as most of the troops committed to such a large-scale raid had been briefed previously for Rutter, the decision had been taken that for the sake of security they should have minimum notice. This lack of notice had also influenced the substitution of paratroopers by commandos, as Commander Airborne Forces had insisted that his troops would need four days' notice. One problem for the Canadians was that in the six weeks since the cancellation of Rutter there had been the usual turnover in manpower of about five percent, and the new replacements were not trained to the same standards as the remainder of the Division.

The 2nd Canadian Division deployed on 'Exercise Ford I' as planned, heading for Portsmouth and Southampton, while the commandos of the Special Service Brigade assembled at Newhaven. Here the landing craft were hidden under a large

**Lord Louis Mountbatten at his best – inspiring the men before battle. In this case addressing commandos at Newhaven on the eve of Jubilee.**

**Canadian soldiers awaiting orders to embark on their landing ships at Portsmouth.**

canvas sheet, and the landing ships to be used by Number 4 Commando had been disguised to look like merchantmen. Canvas screens created extra bulkheads, and additional dummy funnels had been erected to alter their shape totally, as seen by the twelve *Luftwaffe* observation or air-photograph sorties that the Germans tasked over Newhaven on 18 August.

Naval Commando John Mellor wrote:

> *'No. 3 Commando had to*

**Infantry boarding shipping on the afternoon of 18 August 1942.**

queue outside the docks in the streets for half an hour before they could board their boats. The civilians left their houses, and sensing the importance of the occasion, watched in silence from the curb side.'

Further west along the coast, reporter Ross Munro described his embarkation with the Essex Scottish at Portsmouth on the evening of 18 August:

'The port at 6 P.M. was a busy spot. The last truckload of Canadians and their ammunition and equipment were arriving. It caused no particular stir and the workers paid scant attention to the troops, whom they had seen many times before, going and coming on manoeuvres.

'By 7 P.M., I was aboard the Queen Emma, another peacetime Channel vessel turned into an infantry assault ship for combined operations. The Emma carried the headquarters of the Royal Regiment as well as several hundred assault troops, mortar crews and miscellaneous detachments.

'There were sealed envelopes distributed to us all there - the same maps of Dieppe and the same photographs and plans we had hopefully learned to know in every detail in July.

'The officers and men had been told by now that they were going to Dieppe tonight, and there were hurried conferences aboard the ship, refresher briefings and eleventh-hour prep- arations. Few of the Royals seemed to be in as confident a mood as I had known them in "practice Dieppe." The rush to the port, and the mass of detail which had to be crammed again in a few hours, left everyone rather ragged.

**The British Sten gun – cheap and mass produced.**

'Even before we put to sea, some had an ominous feeling about what was ahead of them on the other side of the Channel. Nobody said anything but many were wondering how the security had been in the time since July 7. . . They were puzzled, too, why the raid had been decided upon so suddenly. They would have liked more time to adjust themselves. I shared most of their mental discomfort.'

One point that is made in virtually all infantry accounts is that the crudely manufactured Sten guns, issued to many Canadians in lieu of their rifles on the Isle of Wight, had been withdrawn on the cancellation of Operation Rutter. Now, on the dockside, brand new weapons were being issued to the troops. The Canadians were not happy. They had tuned their 'Rutter Stens' extensively to make the cheaply engineered and hastily manufactured weapons anything like reliable. Corporal Red Sudds of the South Saskatchewan Regiment, boarding HMS *Princess Beatrix* at Southampton explained the problem:

> 'They're a goddamn crude gun to begin with. Mass produced so quickly that rivets are left sticking out, and they can jam. But when you have your own Sten, you file these bits down and polish out the roughness. These goddamn guns were raw, still in the grease they were packed in at the factory. Twenty rounds out of these buggers and they'd jam. That's why I tried to file down what I could. And a lot of other guys were doing the same thing.'

As darkness fell, the force sailed, and assembled off the South Coast as planned. Captain Denis Whitaker aboard the landing ship HMS *Glengyle*, sailing at 2120 hours from Southampton, with the Royal Hamilton Light Infantry, recorded that:

> 'As we sailed out of Southampton harbour that evening, there was absolute silence except for the swishing sound the *Glengyle* made as she slid through an almost perfectly calm English Channel.

**An example of the LCP(L) and its naval crew in Newhaven.**

# HUNT CLASS DESTROYER
## FITTED AS H.Q. SHIP

W/1 EQUIPMENT IN USE. AERIALS ONLY ARE INDICATED
KEY:- (THOSE UNDERLINED WERE PREVIOUSLY FITTED
IN THE SHIP)

(a) T.R. 1133 FIGHTER COVER

(b) T.R. 1133 FIGHTER SUPPORT

(c) Q.H. NAVIGATIONAL AID

(d) MOTOROLA V.H./F INTERCOMMUNICATION

(e) No. 19 – T.A.C. R AND
V.H./F INTERCOMMUNICATION

(f) No. 19 – T.A.C. R AND
V.H./F INTERCOMMUNICATION

(g) No. 12 – SMALL CRAFT B'CAST (FITTED SUBSEQUENTLY)

(h) No. 46 – NAVAL BEACH WAVE

(i) No. 18 – STAND BY SET

(j) No. 19 – L.C.T. BROADCAST

(k) TYPE 60 – SHIP – SHORE

(l) No. 19 – DIV. A

(m) TYPE 60 – ADMIRAL'S WAVE

(n) PHANTOM – RECONNAISSANCE REPORTS

(o) T.R. 1133 – STAND-BY FIGHTER

(p) G.E.C. (7A) – V.H./F INTERCOMM AND TO SHORE
D/F

(q) D/F

(r) R.D.F. – TYPE 285 (RANGING)

(s) R.D.F. – TYPE 286 (WARNING)

(t) PLESSEY – E BOAT INTERCEPTION

ALSO RECEIVING AERIALS NOT SHOW –

(u) BROADCAST H.D.

(v) PORT WAVE

(w) DIV. B WAVE

(x) BRIGADE WAVE(S,

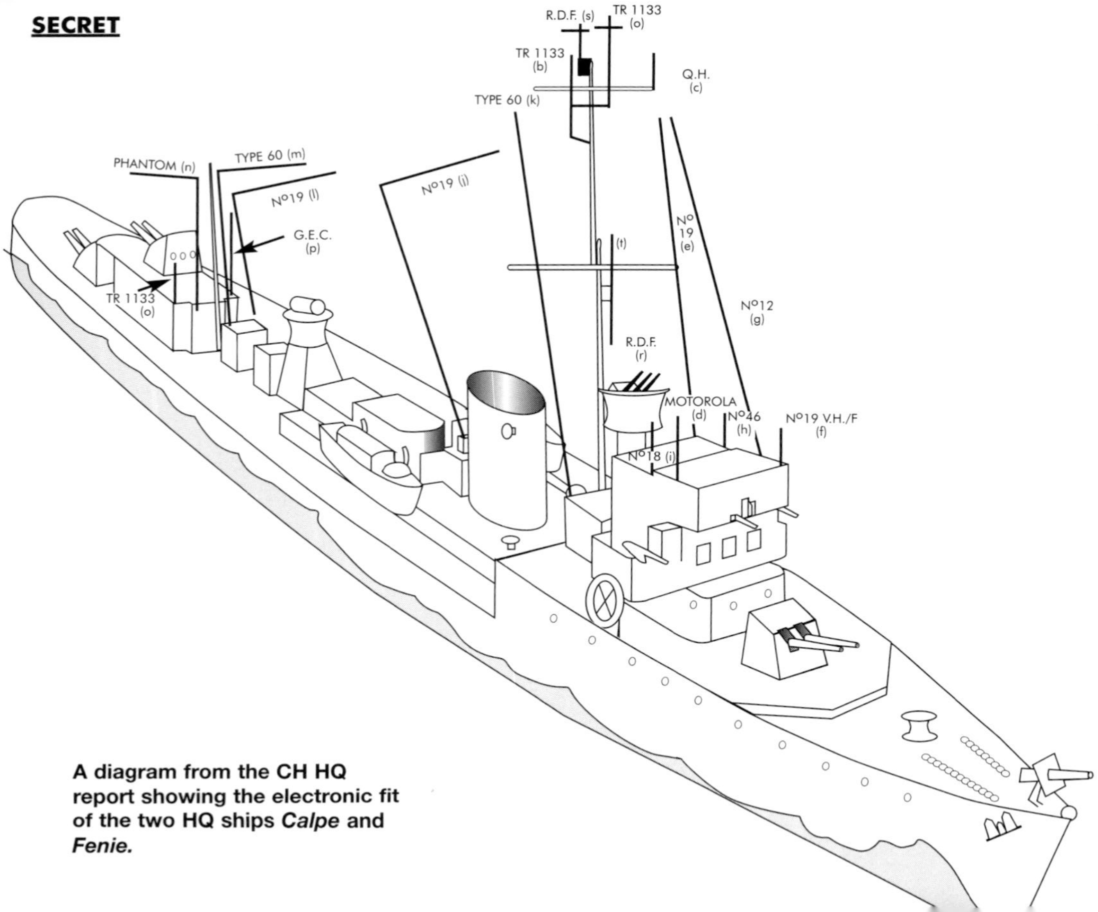

A diagram from the CH HQ
report showing the electronic fit
of the two HQ ships *Calpe* and
*Fenie*.

*We spent the time we had left cleaning weapons, priming grenades, distributing maps and escape kits, and briefing the troops on their tasks. We did our best to prepare them, but the feeling of optimism many of us had shared before Rutter was now being replaced by apprehension.'*

Not all the raiders had the 'luxury' of being able to try to get a little sleep and a hot breakfast in a substantial Landing Ships Infantry (LSI). The Fusiliers Mont-Royal, the Brigade reserve for the main assault on Dieppe, were embarked in R-Craft and Landing Craft Personnel. Crammed in the diminutive craft, a Warrant Officer recalled that 'despite the soporific throb of our own engines, it was difficult for the men sitting upright to get much sleep.'

Aboard HMS *Calpe*, one of the Hunt Class destroyers, converted mainly by adding extra communications equipment to act as Force HQ ship, Major General Roberts and his staff were joined by Air Commodore Cole, who represented the RAF. Also onboard was the Commander of the Naval element of the force, Captain Hughes Hallett, who as part of Combined Ops had done much of the original Rutter planning. Remaining off Dieppe, the force commanders would use *Calpe's* high power radios to transmit back to RAF Uxbridge, where Admiral Mountbatten and General Crerar had joined Air Marshal Leigh-Mallory to monitor the action at his headquarters.

Several thousand miles away in Cairo, Churchill and Field Marshal Alanbrooke were waiting for news, and as usual, Churchill's mood was swinging from exaltation at the prospect of action to the depths of despair. Tension mounted as the reported weather conditions in the Channel hung in the balance. The Prime Minister had made commitments to both the Russians and the Americans, and he needed a military success for the sake of morale at home. Earlier, when questioned about the risks of such an ambitious raid and its place in the war's strategy, Field Marshal Alanbrooke told Churchill that

*'...no responsible general will be associated with any planning for invasion until we have an operation at least the size of an attack on Dieppe behind us to study and base our plans upon.'*

## Naval Action

One of the British planning assumptions, based largely on the performance of their own RDF or radar, was that the Germans cliff-top radar would not spot the Jubilee Naval Force heading south

German radar or RDF stations were springing up all along the coastline to give warning of the approach of enemy aircraft and shipping.

across the Channel to Dieppe. In the event, both German and British radar spotted and reported enemy activity, which if acted on, especially in the case of the British, may well have made a significant difference to the outcome of the raid.

The thirteen groups of the Naval Force assembled, and were 'more or less in their planned positions as they reached the buoys marking the entrance of the swept channel and crossed through the German minefield.' So far, the operation was proceeding much better than during the two Yukon exercises. But they had been spotted by German radar. However, luck was with the Allies: as was often the case, the radar plot had been dismissed as 'either false or it was the *Kriegsmarine* convoy from Boulogne.' There are also reports that information was passed to 302nd *Infanterie* Division, who, it is believed, passed messages reinforcing vigilance among its troops, who were already at their posts, trying to get some sleep. It is worth emphasising that, following a series of radar-inspired false alarms

A flotilla of R Craft leaving Newhaven on the eve of Operation Jubilee.

since May, this was not a general '*Alarmsignal*' and was not acted on as such, but it certainly adds to the emerging picture of subsequent speedy German reaction.

As already mentioned, radar could also have played a significant role in the conduct of the raid on the British side of the Channel. As early as 2130 hours, various Chain Home radar stations detected three enemy vessels off Boulogne, heading south-west towards Dieppe. However, they were at extreme range and 'subject to intermittent fading.' A vague insubstantial warning was sent to the Headquarters embarked on HMS *Calpe*, but the Jubilee Force had already passed the 'point of no return' once it was through the minefield. There is also doubt whether these messages ever reached Jubilee's naval commanders.

Meanwhile, on the eastern flank of the British force, Naval Group 5, made up of eighteen (five had already broken down) Landing Craft Personnel (Large) (LCP(L), also variously known as R Craft or 'Eurekas'), carrying No. 3 Commando to Yellow Beach and the Goebbels Battery. Onboard the accompanying Steam Gunboat 5 (SGB 5) was Captain Barber, who had 'cadged a lift' to Dieppe:

'It all seemed so peaceful. I travelled on the bridge, and was asked to man a Browning machine gun in case of emergency. The steam gunboat was larger than an MGB and had a funnel from which occasionally would belch forth a volley of sparks in a most disconcerting manner. Each time this happened, an absolute tirade of abuse from the Captain would pour down the speaking tube to the engine room and then all would be peaceful for a time. It was after

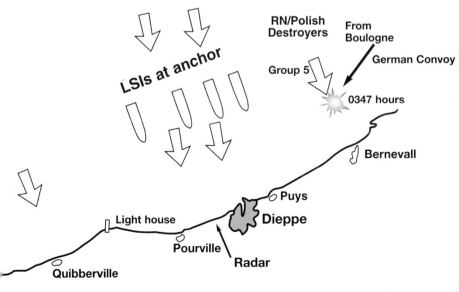

*one of these unnerving explosions of sparks ... that there followed a*
*loud report'*

Thus it was that two hours before the commandos were due to land, British and German naval forces clashed off the French coast. The official report records:

*'At 0347 hours . . . About seven miles from the coast, a ship on*
*the port bow of SGB 5 was observed. Immediately afterwards, the*
*group was lit up by a star shell. Heavy fire from anti-aircraft guns*
*including a few rounds of 3-inch or 4-inch shells was experienced.'*

At first, Group 5's commander, Commander Wyburd RN, thought that the clash could have been the result of mistaken identity by two of the escorting destroyers *Brocklesby* and *Slazak*, who were supposed to be covering the force's left flank. These two ships were in fact off to the north-east, and, amidst much criticism, their Captains explained that their lack of response was due to their belief that the engagement was on land. Meanwhile, 'more enemy ships opened fire on Group 5, and SGB 5 eventually found herself engaged by at least five enemy craft, spreading in an arc from the port to the starboard bow.' These craft were the armed tanker *Franz* and her escort of five E-Boats. The tanker's cannon and the E-Boats' automatic 40mm guns caused significant damage to the lightly armed Group 5. In a matter of minutes, SGB 5 was hit and was almost dead in the water, and six of the light plywood R Craft carrying the commandos were sunk. Many of the other craft scattered into the cover of the darkness and dawn mist. Lieutenant Lewis, aboard LCP 15, recalled the action:

*'The air was filled with the whine of ricochets and the bang of*
*exploding shells, but the flak was flying ahead and astern of us.*
*Putting on full speed we went under the stern of the disabled steam*
*gunboat and tore away from the lashing beams of flack.'*

On board SGB 5, clouds of steam hissed from the fractured pipes, as the boat lost way. Lieutenant Colonel Durnford-Slater recounted:

*'...with the moans of the dying in my ears, I managed to reach the*
*bridge through tangles of wreckage. A shell had scored a direct hit*
*and it was piled with about ten dead and wounded sailors. One*
*badly wounded naval officer cried, "This is the end!" I was inclined*
*to believe him and took off my boots and blew up my Mae West, as*
*it looked as if we would soon be swimming.'*

Despite the naval clash, a small part of Naval Group 5 faithfully executed Commander Wyburd's orders to press on towards France, even though it was obvious that the enemy on the coast would have been alerted. On shore, however, the reaction was patchy. Many infantry units disregarded the naval action as 'a routine event' that had nothing to do with them, although in some headquarters it added to the picture already painted by German radar. What is obvious with hindsight was not necessarily obvious to the tired and bored night-watch-keepers and staff of 571 *Infanterie* Regiment, who may not even have received the details of the radar warning.

Some miles astern of the leading groups, with Naval Group 7, Sergeant Major Dumais of the Fusiliers Mont-Royal recalls hearing the action:

> *'Suddenly there was a noise in the far distance. We listened intently. It was far too early for the assault. The naval officer cut the engine and the boat settled in the water. We all held our breath in an attempt to catch the least sound, but all we could hear was the gentle slapping of waves against the side of the boat. Then from astern, came two short blasts on a siren, and a destroyer emerged from the light fog, only to rush past, full of majesty and chasing with its bow a mass foam…'*

An hour later, off Dieppe, a German tug was waiting to help manoeuvre the tanker into the port of Dieppe. As darkness gave way to nautical twilight, the tugboat's captain saw destroyers and

Dieppe 1942 – COHQ photograph

Basin du Canada

Arriere Port

astern
eadland

Avant Port

Esplanade

smaller craft bearing down on him. This was not what he expected, and he ordered full steam back to port. Meanwhile, the port's naval signal station had been warned of the activity, and had spotted the unidentified and unexpected ships. No response was received from the ships to the recognition signals, and according to the divisional report, 3 Battery, I/302 Artillery Regiment, positioned on the cliffs above Dieppe, opened fire at 0445 hours. The battle for Dieppe had begun in earnest.

As the commandos and the inner flanking attacks went in to assault their objectives, the main force was either completing its passage or waiting off Dieppe. With the first shells passing overhead, Sergeant Major Dumais in an LCP:

*'... began to get everyone busy. We had to shave and wash in seawater; I tried to convince the men that seawater was very good for the gums! In the best tradition, we could not die without a shave and shiny boots. Nobody had a brush, so we had to borrow a rag from one of the sailors.'*

Some of the much-criticised 'Army bull' had brought an air of normality to a platoon of nervous infantrymen who would shortly be in action for the first time, but:

*'A destroyer on our right suddenly opened up with its heavy guns; we felt at last that the pleasant sea voyage of ours had come to an end. The dreamy haze of that August morning had been finally and firmly dispelled; the fighting we had been preparing for for three years was on us.'*

# CHAPTER FOUR

## THE GOEBBELS BATTERY

*'Young soldiers will follow their commanders out of innocence of their hearts.'*

Brigadier Peter Young to generations of
Officer Cadets 1941 - 1975

Number 3 Commando's operation had not started well. Naval Group 5 had lost five of the unit's twenty-three LCPs to breakdown; four were damaged in the encounter with the German convoy; leaving seven craft to press on with a Motor Launch (ML). Another seven were dispersed during the engagement. In addition, the Commanding Officer Lieutenant Colonel JF Durnford-Slatter was marooned on the damaged SGB 5, whose radio had been knocked out during the fighting. It was not until 0630 hours that Commander Wyburd and Durnford Slater managed to find a set working on one of the dispersed LCPs and pass the information to Headquarters on board HMS *Calpe* that '5 Gp dispersed by enemy'.

The plan to assault the Goebbels Battery (Second *Batterie* 770 Coastal *Artillerie* Battalion) had been simple. The main force was to land with the Commanding Officer on Yellow 1 Beach; a secondary force, under the Second-in-Command, Major Peter Young, was to head for the smaller Yellow II Beach, where they would make their way up the cliff under cover of darkness via a path in a steep gully. Once on the cliff top, the force would silently infiltrate around both flanks and attack the battery from the rear: they hoped to achieve surprise.

Even though the bulk of the force had been dispersed, and only a fraction of the 450 commandos were aboard the landing craft heading to the coast,

**Lieutenant Colonel
Durnford-Slater (left) and
Major Young photographed
in Normandy in 1944.**

(left) One of the pre war postcards of Yellow I Beach used to brief the commandos on their task

(Right) A modern picture showing the two exits from Yellow I

Actual    Planned

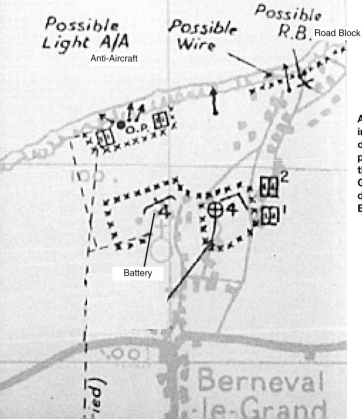

Possible Light A/A
Anti-Aircraft

Possible Wire

Possible R.B. Road Block

O.P.

4

4

2

1

Battery

Berneval -le-Grand

An extract of the intelligence overprint map prepared before the raid, showing German defences in the Berneval area.

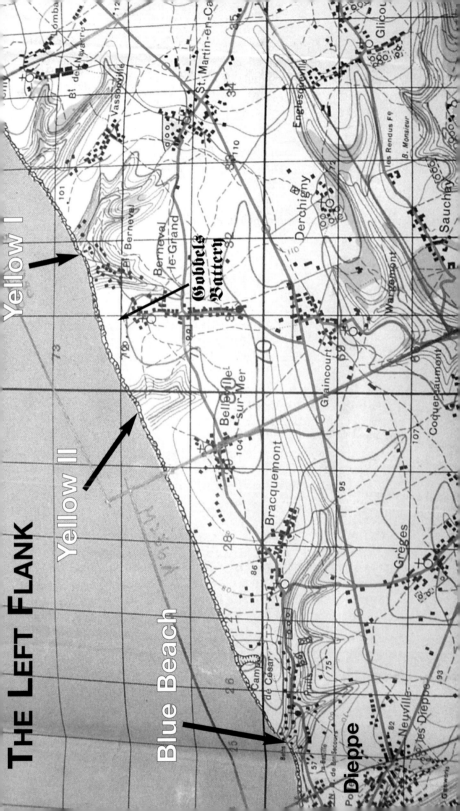

**Landing Craft Personnel (Large) or R Craft photographed during the raid.**

they were determined to carry on with the mission, hoping that more craft would appear out of the darkness.

### Yellow I Beach

Colonel Stacey, the Canadian official historian wrote of No. 3 Commando's main landing:

> 'Certain of the landing craft of Group 5, however, had pushed-on on their own responsibility and made a gallant attempt to complete their task. Five of these landing craft, and subsequently a sixth, reached Yellow I Beach and landed their troops under covering fire from ML 346, five craft touching down at 0510 hrs, 20 mins late.'

The enemy were by now fully alert, however, and to make matters worse, it was virtually full light. Sergeant Dungate recalled after his release from captivity that,

> 'When we were going in you could actually see the defenders standing on the cliffs. The amazing part about it was that they never blew us out of the water but waited until we got right into the beach. You could see the Germans through binoculars watching us come in.'

A German infantry section of ten men from III/571 *Infanterie* Regiment, armed with rifles and a machine gun, were manning their defences, covering the four hundred yards of Yellow I Beach. They opened fire, and both the crafts' crew and commandos suffered casualties as they approached the beach, because the light wooden craft offered virtually no protection from enemy small-arms fire. On board LCP(L) 42, the commandos were given the option to turn back, but they were of one accord: 'We go in!' But as the craft approached the coast, 'The Coxswain had been killed and

YELLOW 1.

This photograph copied from the report shows the intended route off Yellow I Beach as it was prior to the war.

Lieutenant Commander Corke mortally wounded. A trooper of No. 3 Commando took the helm and the troops were landed from the craft when it was in a sinking condition.' Lieutenant Commander Corke, having overseen the transfer of the wounded, went down with his craft.

Meanwhile, on the final run-in to Yellow I, ML 346 and Landing Craft Flak No.1 did their best to suppress enemy positions on the cliff top, in order to cover the landing craft. On the cliff top, a large white house and what appeared to be a small chapel, which were providing cover to the enemy machine gunners, were heavily engaged by ML 346, with 3-pounders, Oerlikon and Lewis guns, and set on fire.

The commandos, consisting mainly of Captain Wills's No.6 Troop, dashed across the beach to the foot of the cliff. Two gullies led up from the beach. The intended route was blocked with coil upon coil of dannert wire, laced with Teller mines on trip wires. Finding a second seemingly less heavily wired gully, Captain Wills set his men to work with wire cutters. Without the sections of tubular ladder, which had been on the craft that did not make it to the beach, it was a slow business, but the commandos forced their way up the cliff. As soon as they reached the top, they came under

fire from a *Spandau*. Captain Wills, originally from the Duke of Cornwall's Light Infantry, was badly wounded, having been hit in the neck. However, two men cleared away the immediate opposition. Corporal 'Banger' Hall, also of the Duke of Cornwall's, charged the enemy machine-gun position single-handed in a 'near-suicidal' charge, dealt with it using grenades, and finished the opposition off with his commando knife. US Ranger Lieutenant Loustalot attacked the second position, but he was not so lucky, and became the first American soldier to be killed in Europe during the Second World War. Reinforced by twenty men from a sixth LCP, the commandos started to push on inland to their objective, even though other enemy positions were still active on the cliff tops. Sergeant Dungate recalled:

*'We did the best we could with what we had, but we were no longer an organized fighting unit after the attack at sea. We had been trained to a pitch for this, but had no plans in case of anything going as badly wrong as this.'*

About fifteen minutes after the initial landing on Yellow I, a sixth LCP landed Lieutenant Dreus and his commandos. It was now full daylight, and enemy machine-gun positions poured bursts of fire into the craft, but ML 346 provided suppressive fire, and a total of thirteen men landed on the beach and scaled the cliff by the route opened earlier by Captain Wills. Lieutenant Dreus and his men provided a welcome reinforcement, bringing the number of men from No. 3 Commando landing on Yellow I to a total of 115. However, with the country offering shorter fields of fire than they had been able to appreciate from maps and photographs, movement towards the battery was slow. Sergeant Dungate continued:

*'We'd been ashore quite a while and hadn't moved very far. I'll never forget it and I remember thinking, "This is not very clever, it's too quiet." We moved out on to a road and there was a tremendous clatter as they opened fire on us. One man called Easterbrook was hit. When we undid his belt, his stomach was in his trousers'*

As the commandos had landed in full daylight, and taken a considerable time to clear the barbed wire and climb the gully, III/571 *Infanterie* Regiment had time to gather troops to reinforce their ten-to-twelve-man cliff-top section, and to call in close air support. First to arrive on the scene was a *Spandau* team sent forward to reinforce the German section. Next were eight men from a nearby *Luftwaffe* post who, lacking infantry training, all fell victim

**German infantry on the clifts above Berneval taken during an exercise prior to the raid.**

to the skilful commandos. Finally, German fighter-bombers raked the cliff tops with cannon fire.

It was not long before the well-rehearsed German counter-attack plans swung into action. Major von Blucher, commander of the divisional reconnaissance and anti-tank battalion, had under command a company of his own men mounted on bicycles and a company of lorried infantry from 570 *Infanerie* Regiment, along with a company of engineers in the infantry role.

Casualties among the commandos mounted, and ammunition was running short. Captain Osmond commented 'We were the only people in the world who were fighting a war, it seemed. We could see and hear all these lorries heading towards us down the road from Dieppe.' The commandos started to withdraw the five hundred yards back to the gully, as the German infantry closed in. Private Grove commented:

> 'We had to lie in the grass, take our turn and dash across the path. I was lucky. They just knocked the heel off one of my boots as I ran for it. Every one of my party got across, but a couple of US Rangers came directly down the path. They hadn't a cat in hell's chance. All we heard was them screaming.'

The wounded Rangers and commandos had to be abandoned and were taken prisoner by the Germans.

Meanwhile, the armed tanker *Franz* had sailed in towards the beach and was engaging the waiting boats and the cliffs. ML 346

**Royal Navy sailors of Motor Launch 346 photographed with the tanker *Franz's* ensign.**

returned the fire and attacked her tormenter, closing to within thirty yards before the ship burst into flames and was driven up the beach. The *Franz's* colours were removed by the British sailors and taken as a battle trophy in spite of fire from the cliff top, which was damaging the waiting craft and causing heavy casualties amongst the Royal Navy crewmen.

The commandos continued to fight their way back to the gully, suffering further casualties. Captain Wills was carried down to the beach by Private Lerigo, whose strength came from hours of hard training on ropes and on the assault course at the Commando Training Centre Achnacarry. When they reached the beach, it was soon apparent that with the enemy firing down from the cliff top there was no prospect of the few remaining wooden LCPs closing into the beach to pick up the surviving commandos. Captain Wills ordered the remaining commandos to head west along the beach to meet up with the Canadians at Puys. But with stick grenades being thrown down the cliff, they were driven into a cave, where they were forced to surrender when German infantry came down onto the beach and fired into the cave. Captain Osmond recalled: 'It was obvious that nobody was coming to collect us, so when the Germans got about twenty yards away, I made everyone pack up.' In the area of Yellow Beach I, thirty-seven men were killed and eighty-two men captured. Only Lance Corporal Sinclair escaped, by swimming out to the LCPs who were being driven further from the beach by enemy fire.

Sergeant Dungate recounted that 'there were masses of Germans. There must have been hundreds of them, all with their bicycles stacked up along the road.' A series of reports confirming the first German success of the day climbed their chain of command, and according to C-in-C West's war diary, von Rundstedt received the news at 1020 hours. However, it was not until he reached Newhaven at about midnight that Lieutenant Colonel Durnford-Slatter discovered that a party of his men under his Second-in-Command had landed at Yellow II and that they had 'an altogether more interesting time ashore in France.'

## Yellow II Beach

What was it that made *Batterie* 2/770 or the Goebbels Battery so special that the commandos would make such determined efforts to continue with their mission? The enemy battery at Berneval le Grand consisted of three 170mm and four 105mm guns, along with anti-aircraft and ground defences manned by more than 120 German gunners and infantry. The 170mm guns were some of the heaviest in this sector of the coast. With a range of almost twenty miles, these guns could cover all the approaches to Dieppe. Even the 105mm guns had a range of almost ten miles and were capable of engaging the stationary Landing Ships Infantry as they disembarked troops into assault craft. If not neutralised, the two types of gun together represented a real and considerable danger to both the Jubilee naval and landing forces

As the two GHQ Phantom signallers and their HF set were aboard one of the LCPs dispersed by the action at sea, there was no one to pass messages back to RAF Uxbridge, where Air Marshal Leigh-Mallory and Lord Mountbatten waited for information. They had to assume that the raid had failed; and it was only later that Durnford-Slater's message 'Force dispersed' was relayed to them via HMS *Calpe*, confirming the worst. However, they had not counted on the determination of the commandos.

At the same time that the five craft were heading for Yellow

Beach I, a lone LCP was heading for the coast under the command of Lieutenant Buckee of the Royal Navy Reserve and Major Peter Young. They

> *'. . . conferred together after the encounter with the convoy, and decided, in spite of this misfortune, to persevere and do their utmost to carry out their task. Accordingly, LCP(L) 15 went into Yellow II Beach, and the party landed without opposition...'*

This single landing craft carried just eighteen commandos - three officers and fifteen men – and landed.

Having decided to continue with the mission, Lieutenant Buckee

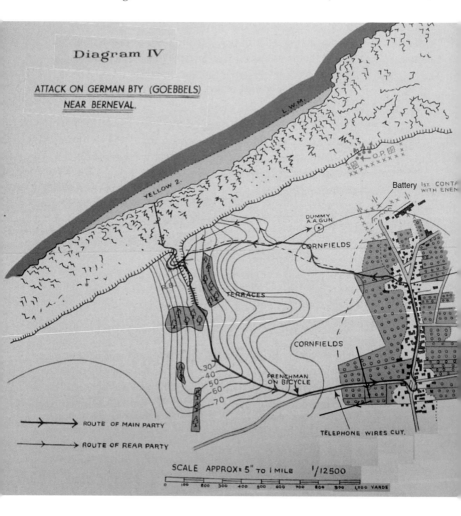

**A sketch map taken from the Combined Operations HQ report showing No. 3 Commando's operations from Yellow Beach II.**

**One of the three French 170mm guns pressed into German service at the Gobbels Battery.**

piloted LCP 15 into the beach five minutes before zero hour. In almost full darkness, with a feat of navigation, he landed Major Young and his seventeen men, undetected by the enemy, within fifty yards of the exit from the narrow Yellow Beach II. The exit via a steep path up a gully was predictably blocked with coils of dannert wire piled ten feet high, and the gully beyond was laced with some particularly vicious-looking barbed wire, pinned to the cliff by stout stakes. Without any means of blowing their way through or cutting the wire, it was going to be a case of forcing and picking their way through. From their small collection of weapons, the group were forced to leave their 3-inch mortar and its four bombs at the base of the cliff. This left them armed with 'one Garand rifle, nine Service rifles [Mark III .303-inch Lee-Enfields], one Bren, six Tommy guns, three pistols [and] one 2-inch mortar with six bombs. . . '

The COHQ report records that:

> 'The gully was climbed by making use of the German wire as a rope and the iron stakes which secured it as a ladder. A rope made by driver J. Cunningham Royal Army Service Corps, out of joined toggle ropes, proved useful at one difficult point.'

Major Young, who admitted he was not a good climber, commented that scaling the cliff was 'rather an ordeal,' and that if faced with attempting it a second time he would have 'reconsidered.' But after some twenty minutes, the small force assembled on the cliff top, cut and bleeding, with uniforms torn. While waiting for the last man to scale the cliff, with the benefit of daylight, Major Young scanned the sea with his binoculars, and was reassured to spot ML 346 and its small gaggle of craft heading for Yellow I. Confident that the original plan was still viable, he later remarked:

> *'Some of the soldiers did not look particularly pleased at the turn of events, so I gave them a pep talk . . . telling them that it would be something to tell their children about.'*

Confidence restored by Peter Young's inspiring personality, they moved inland to the commando rendezvous (RV). The COHQ report recorded:

> *'... on reaching the cliffs, the party moved inland a short distance and took cover in a wood. There, Major Young divided them into three groups, and himself went forward with his runners to reconnoitre. It was decided to make for the village of Berneval in an effort to join with the rest of the Commandos.'*

However, before Young and his group had gone far, the massive guns of *Batterie* 2/770 opened fire on the vulnerable ships lying off Dieppe.

When the commandos reached the Berneval-Dieppe Road, they grabbed a petrified French boy from his bicycle. The frightened lad was on his way to find a doctor to treat his mother, who had been wounded by an RAF bomb that missed its target on the battery, and he confirmed its location and over-estimated its garrison at 200 men. Moving along the road to Berneval, the commandos took the precaution of scaling a telegraph pole and cutting the telephone wires to Dieppe.

Major Young's group reached the edge of the village, just as six Hurribombers from 175 Squadron pitched their 250-pound bombs into the battery. The doubling commandos were greeted by 'about twenty inhabitants, who showed great friendliness, particularly the boys and young men, one of whom pointed out the exact position of the Battery.' Moving more slowly north up the main Berneval-le-Grand street, the commandos passed the local Sappers-Pompier putting out a fire caused by Allied bombing in a house, while the

**The view across the valley from Yellow II Beach towards Berneval-le-Grande showing to route taked by the commandos up to the Dieppe - Berneval Road**

**Plumes of water amongst the Allied ships, thrown up by heavy shell fire shortly after dawn on 19 August 1944**

French boy's wounded mother was evacuated in a wheel-barrow. In spite of this, the French people were not resentful. However, Major Young and his group came under *Spandau* fire from the church tower, which sending flakes of stone, whining around their ears, as wildly-aimed enemy fire struck the buildings above them. With covering fire from Private Anderson's only weapon, a pistol, the group went to ground. Two officers armed with Thompson sub-machine guns returned fire. Neither of these weapons had a realistic chance of hitting the enemy at the range in question, but return fire kept the heads of the *Wehrmacht* coastal infantry down until the 2-inch mortar and its six rounds of high explosive could be brought into action against the church tower. As an area weapon, a light mortar would not normally be the weapon of choice for such a target, but it was all they had available. With skill or luck the

**The rebuilt church at Berneval and the area where the commandos come under fire**

commandos, having fired several rounds, knocked-out the *Spandau* with a direct hit by an HE bomb. The COHQ report states:

> 'An attempt was then made to climb the belfry, from the top of which it would have been possible to snipe the Battery effectively with the Bren gun. There were no stairs, however, or other means of climbing to the top, and this plan was perforce abandoned. Major Young then made his way through an orchard, passing a dummy AA gun, into cornfields; here desultory sniping fire was opened on our men.'

All this time, the battery, probably with only a single gun in action, was engaging the landing ships off Dieppe 'at a very slow rate' of fire. It is estimated that 'the number of rounds got off was not more than twenty.' The reason that only a single gun was firing is not known, but we can speculate that the RAF bombing had knocked out or damaged the guns or otherwise neutralised some of the gun crews. Whatever the reason, it could surely only be a matter of time before more guns came into action. Although the remainder of No 3 Commando, who had been seen heading for Yellow I, had failed to arrive, Major Young recalls that his group's rapid advance into the village, and a 'dose of enemy fire', had restored his men's morale:

> 'They had now got their blood up and quite recovered their spirits. They were beginning to enjoy themselves . . . There seemed to me to be no future in advancing against a hidden enemy, and it occurred to me that we might be better off in the cornfields . . . In the Army, you are told that two bricks will stop a bullet. I announced that nine feet of corn would stop a bullet. Fortunately, my soldiers believed this, or appeared to. We ran into the cornfield and opened a fairly heavy fire on the battery, but not rapid because I hadn't got much ammunition.'

Reconciled to the fact that they were on their own, the commandos worked their way forward to within two hundred yards of the battery and, at nearly 0630 hours, they opened fire on the German gunners. Deliberately dispersed, Major Young's small command did their best to simulate a larger force, by firing and crawling back out of sight before dashing to a new fire position. As a result of their small-arms fire, the German gunners were prevented from serving their guns, as they would have had to stand up in their open concrete gun positions.

At this stage, commandos were thwarted in their attempt to close right up to the battery when ML 346, waiting off Yellow

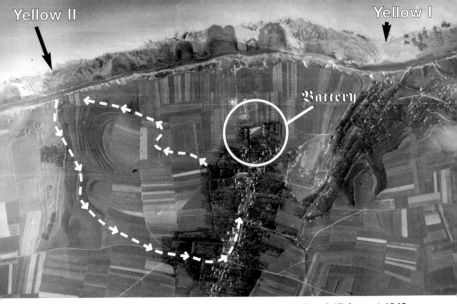

**Air photograph of the Yellow Beaches and Berneval areas dated 17 August 1942**

Beach, opened fire on Goebbels Battery with her diminutive 3-pounder gun. Although the high-explosive content was relatively small, the friendly shell splinters also kept the commandos back at a respectful distance.

Eventually the German gunners traversed one of the 170mm guns inland, and the commandos saw the gun being depressed to engage them. When the gun fired, it was apparent that it could not depress sufficiently to engage Major Young's commandos, and the shell passed overhead to explode about a mile inland. Fire was returned by shooting into the gun's 'black and yellow fumes,' which drove the gunners to cover; thereafter, until 0730 hours, they kept the enemy gunners' heads down. However, with little ammunition, with German reinforcements no doubt on the way, and with such a small force under his command, Major Young sent Captain Selwyn 'back to form a bridge-head on the beach, with orders to fire three white Verey lights if an LCP was available for evacuation. These were presently seen to burst in the sky.'

It was not to be a headlong dash to the beach: that would be an invitation to be overwhelmed

Air photography and the resulting intelligence overprints had a long way to go before they reached the standards of those issued to D Day troops.

**The Army Commandos fought under their own parent regiments cap badge**

by the Germans, who had to be keep at a respectful distance, while the commandos 'leap-frogged' back to the beach from fire position to fire position. As they approached the cliff, Lieutenant Ruxton, Trooper About and Major Young gave covering fire with the Bren gun, while the remainder made their way through the wire. On reaching the gully down to the beach, Lance Corporal White, a commando volunteer from the Devon Regiment, stepped on a mine; but despite his terrible wound, he recovered the 3-inch mortar that had been abandoned on the beach, and successfully fired all four available rounds at the battery. This, in the finest traditions of his regiment and the commando spirit, he did under his own initiative.

At 0737 hours, Lieutenant Bukee very bravely ordered his coxswain to take LCP(L) 15 into Yellow I Beach, under the heavy covering fire provided by ML 346, who kept the Germans on the cliff top at bay. This fire enabled the now-vulnerable commandos to struggle into the sea, taking the wounded Lance Corporal White with them. Lieutenant Ruxton, with his Bren gun resting on top of his Mae West lifejacket, Trooper About and Major Young were the last three men to reach the landing craft at about 0810 hours. According to the ship's log, at 0820 hours, LCP(L) 15 was 'withdrawing under the cover of smoke and returning to England, being unsuccessfully attacked by a Ju 88 at 1045 hours.'

Major Young and the eighteen commandos on this single craft were the only ones among No. 3 Commando who landed on Yellow Beach I and II who reached the UK, less Lance Corporal Sinclair. They rejoined the remainder of Lieutenant Colonel Durnford-

**R Craft heading north back to England.**

Slater's No. 3 Commando at Newhaven. The men left at Yellow Beach I, mostly wounded, became prisoners of war.

The COHQ report summarised the operations at Yellow Beach:

*'So much for the attempt to capture and destroy the "Goebbels" Battery to the east of Dieppe. It was not crowned with success, but there is no doubt that the sniping tactics employed by Major Young and his men greatly interfered with the handling of the battery for upwards of an hour and a half, during the critical period of the landing.'*

**Major Peter Young (centre) and some of his men celebrate their success with navy rum during the passage home.**

To the success of the commandos must be added a reminder that the six Hurribombers of 175 Squadron probably also played a significant part in neutralizing the Goebbels or *Batterie* 2/770 on the morning of 19 August 1942.

**Soldiers of 3 Commando pose for photographs on the quay side at Newhaven on the morning of 20 August 1942.**

# CHAPTER FIVE

## OPERATION CAULDRON

*'Commandos - Churchill's rats who kill by night.'*
Signal 1942

The second of the major coastal batteries that the commandos attacked during the preliminary operations lay five miles west of the port. Code-named Hess by the British, it lay about a thousand yards inland from the cliffs, near the village of Varengeville, and it was capable of covering the sea approaches to Dieppe. COHQ described the battery as 'together with Goebbels, constituting the most important part of the defence of Dieppe.' This was to be the objective of Lieutenant Colonel The Lord Lovat's No. 4 Commando. Their mission was to destroy the guns before they could come into action against the Canadians, who would be disembarking at dawn from the landing ships into their assault craft.

Hess Battery, commanded by *Hauptmann* Scholer, was in fact the *Wehrmacht* 813 *Batterie*, consisting of six 150mm guns designed pre-war specifically for coastal defence. It was sited to engage shipping off Dieppe at a range of 8,600 yards, which was well within the battery's maximum range of seventeen miles. Intelligence

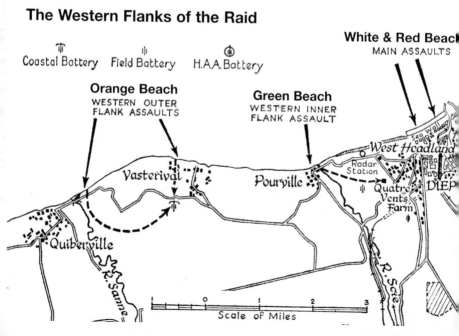

## The Western Flanks of the Raid

translated the battery's orders captured during the raid: one specific task read, 'On receipt of the order *"Sperrfeuer* Dieppe" six rounds per gun are to be fired.' This single fire mission of thirty-six rounds would be the foretaste of things to come once the battery ranged on Allied shipping.

In February 1942, work had begun on improving the battery position, and by August, each of the six guns was positioned in an open concrete gun pit and mounted on a platform that enabled engagements to be carried out over a full 360 degrees. Five of the guns were in single line, while the sixth was located some distance from the main battery. The Germans had put considerable resources into the air and ground defence of the battery, but despite this, at the time of the raid the *Kriegsmarine* were pressing for the battery to be relocated to a less vulnerable position within the defended perimeter of Dieppe. At the battery, the commandos were

**(Above) Construction of a gun pit for a 150mm coastal on the Atlantic Wall. Note the use of slave labour from eastern Europe.**

**(Left) Three of the Hesse Battery's guns, photographed in their concrete gun pits.**

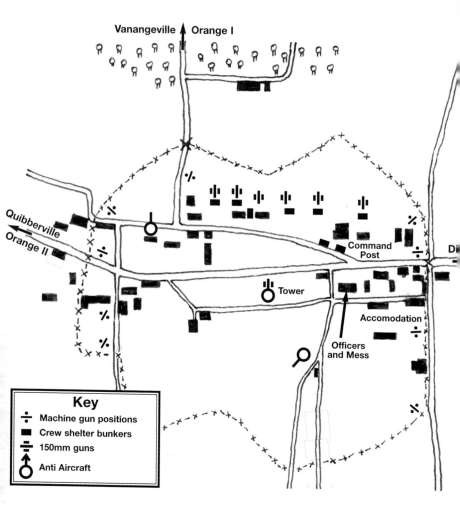

to face a dual-purpose 20mm anti-tank/anti-aircraft gun and a further two 20mm anti-aircraft guns, one of which was mounted in a ten-metre-high flak tower immediately behind the main gun position. The battery observation post manned by *Kriegsmarine* coastal gunnery specialists was in a cliff-top lighthouse between the two beaches that No. 4 Commando was to use for landing.

The ground defences consisted of nine half-section posts, each of four or five men under a junior NCO, based on light machine gun. Covering relatively open fields of fire out to 200 to 300 yards, two of these positions were of concrete construction, while the remainder were placed in ordinary revetted field defences. Altogether, the commandos were told that they could expect to encounter up to five hundred *Kriegsmarine* gunners and marine infantry: the garrison numbered somewhat over a hundred men. 813 *Batterie* was surrounded by a double barbed-wire fence and it was expected that the gap between the two fences would be sown with anti-personnel mines.

## Training

Despite the seemingly sudden change of plan, in which the commandos took over responsibility for the preliminary attacks from airborne forces, the experienced commandos were essentially well prepared. Now under the command of a new breed of leader, both No. 3 and 4 Commandos went into a period of intensive, tough and realistic training. Fitness was honed, along with skill at arms. After they had been given all available details of the battery, task-specific training was organised, such as placing demolition charges to ensure destruction of gun positions. No 4 Commando returned to Dorset to be billeted in houses at Weymouth, where in spite of posters reminding the locals that walls have ears, their comings and goings were the subject of some discussion. In the harbour and bay, they trained on boats and used the Isle of Purbeck cliffs to practise climbing. Individual components of the raid gradually came together as the commando repeatedly 'raided' the cliff tops around Lulworth Cove. The whole package culminated in a 'raid' on a position inland from Whorbarrow Bay, but, as in the case of the Canadian Yukon exercises, there were navigational difficulties. Sailing in the dark, from the point where they transferred into their assault craft some ten miles off shore to a small bay at the foot of the Dorset cliffs, proved to be a significant challenge. However, after

(Above) Hard physical training both in its own right and during tactical exercises created robust soldiers

(Left) Cliff climbing was an important part of commando training

improvements in the navigational arrangements, No. 4 Commando was ready.

## The Commando Plan

Lord Lovat's plan for his 265 officers and soldiers (including a photographer), plus a handful of US Rangers and Free French commandos, was similar to that of No. 3 Commando. He said, 'My task was fundamentally: in and out – smash and grab.' Lovat planned to split his force into two groups, who would attack the battery respectively from the front and the rear. His Second-in-Command, Major Derek Mills-Roberts, led Group 1, which was to be the fire support group, landing on Orange Beach 1 at Vasterville. This group consisting of C Troop, a section of A Troop, the 3-inch mortar Section, the 2-inch mortar and Boys Anti-tank rifle sections. Their task was to advance on the battery to a point where they could bring it under effective fire in order to cover Group 2's assault. Lieutenant Colonel Lord Lovat and the remainder of the commando forming Group 2 would land to the east of the River Saane at Quiberville, which was known as Orange Beach II. While Major Mills-Roberts and his party would engage the enemy from the front, with small arms and mortars, Lovat's Group 2, consisting of 164 men (B and F Troops and a section of A Troop), would

double-march on a route up *la Vallee Saane* and approach the battery from the south-western flank. 'The intention then was to carry the battery by storm, by the speed, fury and surprise of an attack from the rear.' As already mentioned, Group 2 would attack with the covering fire of Major Mills-Roberts's group, which included 3-inch mortar HE and smoke. Coordinated with the assault was an air strike by a total of twelve cannon-firing Spitfires of 129 Squadron, flying out of Thorney Island.

Once taken, the Hess Battery was to be destroyed by commando-trained Royal Engineers of F Troop, who were to carry heavy packs of explosives throughout the raid. Meanwhile, the command post was to be rifled for anything of intelligence interest. C Troop was to form a beachhead

86

**Lieutenant Colonel The Lord Lovat, Commanding Officer of No. 4 Commando**

Orange II

R. SAANE

Lt. Col. Lord Lovat
1 Sect. of 'A' Troop
B Troop, 'F' Troop
H.Q.

EAST END OF CLIFFS

MAIN ASSAULT

STE. MARGUERITE

H.Q. Lt. Col. Lord Lovat

POINTE D'AILLY

VASTERIVAL

VARENGEVILLE

Orange I

MAJ. MILLS ROBERTS
SECTION OF 'A' TROOP
AND 'C' TROOP

A.A. GUNS          TELEPHONE
                   WIRE
HEAVY GUNS    XXXXXXX
              BARBED
STRONG        WIRE
POINTS

at Orange Beach I., through which the whole of the Commando would withdraw.

## Orange Beach II

No. 4 Commando was embarked on HMS *Prince Albert* – a former Belgian cross-Channel ferry, pressed into service as a Landing Ship Infantry (Small). Accompanying them was Steam Gun boat 9 (SGB *Grey Goose*) skippered by Lieutenant Peter Scott, later a renowned ornithologist and artist. He recalled:

> 'A warm wind was blowing from the French coast, laden with the smell of hayfields but I could not yet see the land. . . It flashed three times, then twenty seconds later it flashed three times again. The Germans had left their lighthouse burning to guide us. Then we were achieving surprise!'

According to the ship's log, *Prince Albert* hove-to at 0258 hours, some seven miles from the coast. The commandos disembarked into seven Landing Craft Assault (LCA). These craft were larger than the R Craft used by No. 3 Commando, and could carry about thirty men each: their upper works were lightly armoured, offering protection against small arms and shell splinters. With the lighthouse flashing away, the landing-craft flotilla's commander, Lieutenant Commander Mulleneux, had an easier navigational task than was anticipated, especially after the exercise off the Dorset coast! He later modestly commented that this was 'thanks largely to the fact that Point d'Ailly showed for about five minutes every quarter of an hour, and that the harbour lights of Dieppe were kept burning.'

**An extract from the 1:50k map covering 4 Commando's area of operation**

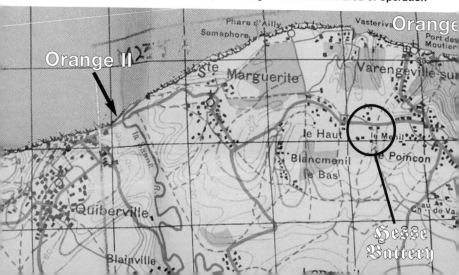

At 0350 hours, only just after star shells glimmered on the horizon to the east as No 3 Commando encountered the tanker and her escort, No. 4 Commando's straightforward run-in was nearly compromised. Another German convoy of three vessels was heading east to Dieppe under cover of darkness: it was probably for their benefit that the lighthouse was operating. Lieutenant Commander Mulleneux and his crew spotted the ships, and 'considered it prudent to evade... The course of the flotilla was therefore altered fairly drastically to starboard in order to pass well clear and astern of the suspicious vessels.' Having luckily avoided sharing what would have been a similar fate as No. 3 Commando, the small flotilla pressed on, divided into their two groups at the appointed spot two miles from the coast, and headed for the Orange Beaches.

The final twenty minutes of the run-in to Quiberville Beach (Orange II) were uneventful. The roar of Rolls-Royce engines broke the stillness, as two cannon-firing Spitfires from 129 Squadron dived on the lighthouse observation post and its two 36mm anti-aircraft guns. The evidence of digging around the lighthouse on air photos had led COHQ intelligence officers to overestimate the defences, hence the perceived necessity of neutralising the OP area. According to Lieutenant Peter Scott aboard the *Grey Goose*, the net result was that:

'. . . streams of . . . white tinselly tracer went up from the battery round the lighthouse, which seemed to consist of about five guns. To the eastward along the coast was more tracer, but all going upwards – still the landing craft were undetected.'

Even with the coastal positions fully alert (and now located by the commandos) it was not until the craft were approaching Orange Beach II that Lovat's landing craft were spotted. Flares arced into the sky from pillboxes overlooking the beach at Quiberville. However, with admirable timing, a second attack by three spitfires served to distract the enemy, and the leading flight of landing craft touched down exactly at Zero-Hour, about twenty yards apart. However, the commandos of A Troop were soon under fire from several *Spandaus* as they dashed across the shingle of the beach to the low cliffs. Here Lieutenant Vasey's men fitted together their lightweight tubular steel ladders and were soon up the eastern cliff, heading for two pillboxes. Lieutenant Scott wrote:

'The pillbox at the eastern end of Orange II opened fire along the beach, and the fire was returned by the Landing Craft Support. The

> *Huns behind the beach fired a six-star green firework – no doubt an*
> *invasion signal – and the party was on!'*

The machine-gun fire was coming from just one of the pillboxes. Two commandos fell wounded as the leading section fought its way forward. A further two were hit as they reached grenade-throwing distance. The first position was knocked-out with well placed No. 36 Grenades. Sergeant Stempson, one of two US Rangers attached to A Troop, spotted a German dashing towards the second pillbox with an ammunition carrier. Stempson opened fire and later commented that 'when you hit them, they rolled over like jackrabbits.'

Meanwhile, Lord Lovat and the second flight of landing craft touched down on Quibberville Beach, further to the west, near the mouth of the River Saane. Under fire from machine guns and mortars, the Commanding Officer described Orange II as 'a nasty beach, quite a steep affair, and the wire on the top of it in the half-light looked almost as high as a ceiling.' Under these conditions, the threat that any man who went to ground on the beach would have his name taken and be 'returned to unit' once back in England, seemed superfluous. However, Lovat justified his threats:

> *'If we had hesitated on that beach, as some do when they get*
> *windy, and flop down, we would have been in trouble. When that*
> *happens with bad troops, you've had it, you can't get them up again.*
> *But these men really tore the wire apart in a way which I can't*
> *believe was possible, looking back on it. They rolled about in it and*
> *went through like loose forwards following a rugger ball.'*

**The point on Orange Beach II where, Lord Lovat's Group landed. The large casemate fallen on the beach is a later war replacement to the 1942 position.**

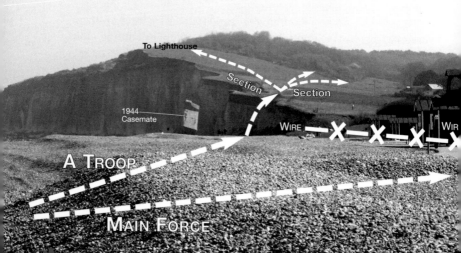

The memorial marking the point where the commandos forced their way through the German wire.

Through sheer determination, the commandos had forced their way through piles of dannert coils fifteen feet deep. A breaching – or rather flattening – team, wearing leather jerkins and carrying rolls of hessian sacking and chicken wire, made a path through the fence. However, mortar fire thinned their numbers, and other commandos dived into the fray and with their bodies produced a viable route through the wire. Group 2 were off the beach.

One unexpected victim of the struggle through the wire was Troop Commander Lieutenant Gilchrist's battle-dress trousers. Snagged on barbs as the wearer forced his way through the clutching coils, his braces broke, and the officer's trousers fell down and he dashed inland 'clutching trousers in one hand, Tommy gun in the other.'

At this point, enemy machine-gun fire switched to the LCAs, who represented an easier target while they withdrew from the beach under clouds of smoke. The Germans had clearly failed to impress on their men the importance of priority targets: in this situation, empty landing craft could not be regarded as a priority. Meanwhile, mortar shells began to fall on a virtually deserted beach. Though the main body of the commandos were through the wire obstacle, Lord Lovat left on the beach a group of medics to treat casualties, and Lieutenant Vasey's section of A Troop, who were to dominate the cliffs to the east of the beach. Sadly, those left on the beach were taken prisoner or were killed, in some cases by friendly fire.

One of Lieutenant Vasey's tasks was to cut telephone wires in order to deny the Germans communication along the coastline. In a pre-planned action, Trooper Finney climbed onto the shoulders of Trooper Brady to reach the top of a telegraph pole and cut the wires. The pair were seen and engaged by the German infantry, but despite rounds smacking into the pole and cracking past their heads, neither man was hit. Trooper Finney was awarded the Military Medal for his part in paralysing this section of the German coastal communications network that relied heavily on fixed line rather than radio.

## Orange Beach I

Two miles out, Major Mills-Roberts's group of three LCAs separated from the main force, with Lord Lovat's wishes for 'good luck' called out across the sea. A *Herald* reporter, AB Austin, who was accompanying the raid, wrote:

*'As we nosed in under the Dieppe cliffs, I heard a Commando whisper to his mate, "Don't forget the other bastards is twice as scared as you." One question worried all of us in those last silent twenty minutes after the long cramped voyage in the starlight. Would the Germans be ready for us? The thought of it made me hang, in my rising funk, on to the thoughts that the "other bastards" were twice as scared as I. A sergeant crouching in front of me kept up a whispered running commentary: "About 500 yards now... see the cliffs? ...There's the crack we want... Look at the Jerry tracer bullets. Don't think they're firing at us though... hundred yards now... fifty."'*

Heading for an ill-defined cleft in the cliff at Varengeville, Lieutenant Commander Mulleneux landed the force at exactly the correct point, undetected by the enemy, even though he spotted a figure on the cliff top! Group 1 touched down only three minutes late. However, they found the eastern gully so choked with barbed wire that they could not get through. Time was passing, and the sky grew gradually lighter: the commandos had to get inland to cover the attack on the battery. So Major Mills-Roberts gave permission to use two Bangalore torpedoes to blow a way up via a second gully, which contained steps for peace-time bathers. Major Mills commented that 'I realised it was likely to sacrifice surprise, but progress otherwise was impossible and time was paramount.' The gully was about twenty feet wide, and beyond it, a long narrow valley ran inland towards some woods that sheltered the shuttered villas of the seaside community of Vasterival-sur-Mer. However, the detonation of the Bangalore Torpedo did not produce an immediate reaction from the enemy, who were spread too thinly to guard every gully up from a possible landing beach.

With the words of Sergeant Major

**The cleft in the cliffs that backed Orange Beach. It was successfully located by Commander Mulleneux on the run in.**

**An LCA touches down on Orange I Beach just after dawn.**

Dunning to 'Get a bloody move on!' ringing in their ears, Captain Dawson's Troop struggled through mud and the shredded wire and on up the steps. At 0520 hours, the two sections moved inland via the valley and began to search the houses of Vasterival. Following them were the mortar section and Major Mills-Roberts's headquarters. As they went up the valley, the commandos spotted an unoccupied position on the spur between the two gullies. There has been some speculation that the figure seen on the cliff was a sentry who had abandoned his position when he saw the LCAs approaching. It is also thought that an isolated rifleman who took pot shots at the troop could have been this man. He was clearly not a sniper, as he was promptly 'killed as he broke cover.'

Meanwhile, Lieutenant Carr and his section of A Troop were heading west to cut the lighthouse OP's telephone cable. However, the Germans may already have passed their fire control orders, as 813 *Batterie* opened fire on the main landing force, now clearly visible out to sea. Major Mills-Roberts wrote:

'Our orders were that the battery had to be knocked out by 6.30 a.m. The convoy appeared to be well ahead of schedule. There was no doubt about this: all the operation orders for the raid had been written ones, and ours were in strict conformity with the main plan. Fifty minutes had been clipped from our very close timetable. It was no good cursing some erratic staff work on the part of someone outside our orbit - the only thing to do was to improvise as fast as possible. Our plan had been to search the houses and ground between the cliffs and the battery. Now it was imperative that we cut this out and reach the battery at once. It would be another fifty

RIVER LA SOANE

MAIN ASSAULT

ST MARGUERITE

SEC. OF 'A' TROOP

PILLBOXES

ORANGE BEACH TWO

L' COL THE LORD LOVAT HC
1 SECT" OF 'A' TROOP, 'B'
TROOP - 'F' TROOP H.Q.

NOT TO SCALE
From a sketch by TPR Mullen
No. 4 Commando

BLANCMENIL
LE BAS

H.Q.

'B' TROOP

'F' TROOP

LE POINCON

MG
MG

FLAT TOWER

LIGHTHOUSE
O.P.

LT. CARR

SECT"
'A' TP

'C' TROOP
CAPT DAWSON

MINED &
WIRED

MORTAR O.P.
FORCE BATTLE

HQO

VARENGEVILLE
SUR MER

MG's

ORANGE BEACH ONE
MAJOR MIL

PORT DES MOUTIERS

DIEPPE

*minutes before Lovat's party could get round by the Saane Valley
and be in their forming-up position prior to the assault.'*

Major Mills-Roberts, his mortar officer, and their signallers 'raced up through the wood,' gathering Lieutenant Style's section from their houses-searching as they went. The battery fired six deafening salvoes in close succession. However, the route through the wood was:

> *... heavy going, as the undergrowth was waist high: the only advantage was that no one else appeared to have used it for a long time... Any idea of pushing through the undergrowth with stealth was out, and we were crashing ahead like a herd of elephants.'*

Suddenly the cover gave way. They were at the edge of the wood and topping a rise, Mills-Roberts and his men came face to face with the battery:

> *'Ennis and I dropped; so did the others. We worked our way forward to a patch of scrub, some fifty yards in front of the wood and about a hundred yards from the perimeter wire of the battery. There was a good view from here, and we heard the words of command distinctly as the battery fired another salvo.'*

From this exposed position, they spotted a barn off to the right. Returning to the cover of the wood, Major Mills-Roberts collected a pair of snipers from Lieutenant Styles' troop, and as they broke into the building, they:

> *'... had a magnificent view of the six big guns and the crews serving them, and had just time to see the three right-hand guns fire a salvo. We ordered one of the snipers to get ready, and pointed out his target. He settled himself on a table, taking careful aim. These Bisley types are not to be hurried; we waited whilst he took the first pressure... At last the rifle cracked; it was a bull's-eye, and one of the Master Race took a toss into the gun pit.'*

The Germans were 'shocked and surprised,' and soon the remainder of Lieutenant Styles' commandos, deployed in covered positions around the barn, joined the sniping at a range of just 170 yards from the battery with their SMLE rifles and Bren guns. The German gunners were driven into the cover of their concrete positions. Mills-Roberts wrote:

> *'It was up to us to see that they did not load again either to shell the main convoy or to attempt to destroy the smaller fry to their front... we didn't relish the idea of having those six-inch guns turned on us.'*

Among Major Mills-Roberts Group were two US Rangers. Corporal

One of the first US soldiers in action in Europe, Ranger Corporal Koons photographed at a medal presentation after the raid.

Koons is credited with being the first American soldier to kill a German in Europe during the Second World War. Taking up a position in the barn with his Garand rifle, he 'found a splendid spot for sniping, just over the manger, and I fired through a slit in the brick wall.'

However, it was not the battery's main armament that was turned on the commandos, but the 20mm anti-aircraft guns and a mortar baseline located some way inland. 'One could see streams of phosphorescent shells as they raked the edge of the wood and the noise as they exploded against tree trunks.' There was little that the commandos could do about the mortars, whose bombs were now exploding all around them, but bringing forward the Boys Anti-tank Rifle Section they took on the anti-aircraft guns. 'Gunner McDonald was firing the gun, with Private Davis as his No 2, and he operated against the flak tower with great effect... Then he devoted his attentions to the German machine guns, ably assisted by the Brens.'

The commando's diminutive 2-inch mortars were in action, but radio communication with the more effective 3-inch medium mortar in the valley by the gully had failed. After one 2-inch ranging shot, the third mortar bomb hit No. 1 Gun's propellant charge bags, 'which ignited with a stupendous crash, followed by shouts and yells of pain.' Sergeant Major Dunning said 'It was luck,

The view from Major Mills Roberts's position at the edge of the wood looking due south towards Hesse battery. The gunpits are marked.

*Left:* Lieutenant General A. G. L. McNaughton, CB, CMG, DSO, Commander in Chief of the First Canadian Army. Before it was agreed that the Canadians were employed in the Dieppe Raid he studied the plan and satisfied himself that it was feasible, given the assurances made by Combined Operations HQ.

*Bottom:* Churchill tanks on manoeuvres in Britain. Churchills were used by the Calgary Regiment on the Dieppe Raid.

Let's Go... CANADA!

The architect of the raid: Vice-Admiral Lord Louis Mountbatten, GCVO, DSO, with his staff at Combined Operations Headquarters. He was appointed as Chief of Combined Operations in April 1942. He is seen here at his headquarters with Major General J. C. Haydon, DSO, OBE and Air Vice-Marshal James Milne Robb, CB, DSO, DFC.

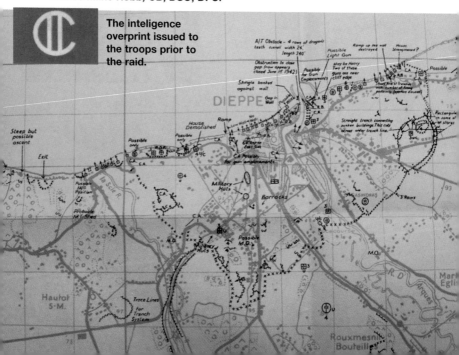

The inteligence overprint issued to the troops prior to the raid.

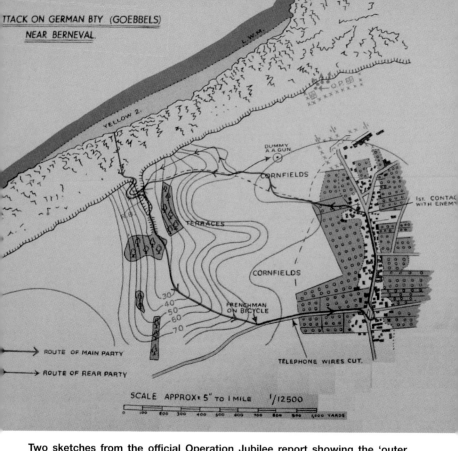

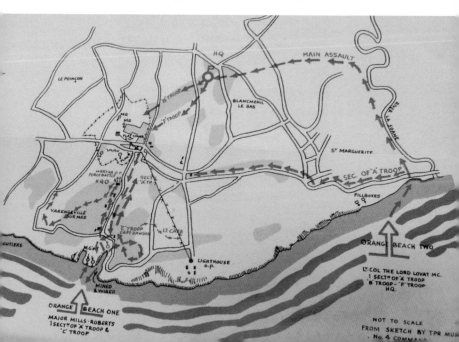

**Drowned and knocked out Churchills photographed by the Germans after the battle.**

**The German view of the Dieppe Raid.**

CIMETIÈRE DES ALLIES

nothing more than luck... probably the luckiest mortar shot of World War II.' The COHQ report recorded that 'the Battery never fired again; up to that moment, it had fired a few salvos which fell into the sea without doing any damage.'

The commandos continued to direct their fire at any German attemps to man the guns or to rescue the wounded. Meanwhile, the heavier weapons suppressed the enemy machine guns, which repeatedly attempted to come back into action. Against the odds, the commandos were winning the firefight, but were doing so at the cost of a steady stream of casualties, mainly due to enemy mortar fire.

While the firefight was going on, the signallers were sending messages back to Major General Roberts on HMS *Calpe* and via the Phantom radio operators on Orange Beach I direct to Admiral Mountbatten at RAF Uxbridge. With a Situation Report transmitted, Mills-Roberts pondered the overall situation:

*'So far so good. But I was desperately anxious to know how Lovat's main assault force was getting on in their wide detour round the flank. We had been unable to get them on the air and did not even know if they had got ashore all right. Otherwise it would be our task also to carry out the assault on the battery at 6.30 a.m. after the cannon fighters had raked it with their guns at 6.28 a.m.'*

However, probably as Group 2 came up out of the Saane Valley, Major Mills-Roberts 'received a signal... confirming that they [Group 2] were now actually in their forming-up position behind the battery.' Group 1 intensified its fire but it remained 'accurate and well-controlled.' Belatedly, communications back to the 3-inch mortar line were established, and they joined the action 'with a heartening crash. At 6.25 a.m. we deluged the whole battery area with smoke and saw the cannon fighters roar in for their two-minute strike at 6.28 a.m. Then we saw the Verey-light signal for the assault by Group 2.'

## The Assault

Lord Lovat led his men through the wire at the back of Orange Beach 2, into cover and out of the field of fire of the Germans' cliff-top positions in the Quibberville area. They had achieved this in a matter of minutes, with minimal casualties from *Spandau*, rifle and mortar fire. Off shore, Lieutenant Peter Scott's *Grey Goose* returned the fire with her three-inch gun. Even as late as 0849 hours, a German Fifteenth Army signal read that 'Around Quiberville the

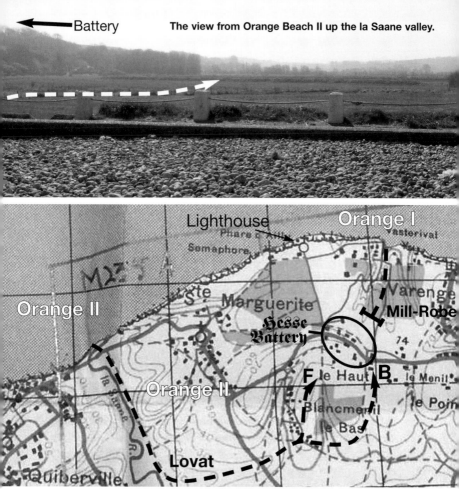

Battery ← The view from Orange Beach II up the la Saane valley.

Lighthouse — Phare
Semaphore
Orange I — asterival
M2 5
Orange II
Ste Marguerite
Varenge
Mill-Robe
Hesse Battery
74
Orange II
F le Haut B le Menil
Blancmesnl le Poin
le Bas
Lovat
Quiberville

situation is not clear and it has not yet been established whether Quiberville has been attacked or not.' The speed of the move off the beach and Corporal Finney's wire cutters had done their job and contributed to success.

The commandos of Group 2 ran a mile inland across rough country along the eastern flank of the Saane valley. Lovat noted:

*'Although we went through German infantry on both sides, we weren't shot at once we had left the beach. We ran the whole dammed way, just stopping occasionally to regroup but nobody got out of breath and we didn't have to wait for laggards.'*

Group 2 turned east up a valley towards the hamlet of Blancmesnl and on towards the battery, which was still over a mile away. At about 0530 hours, Lord Lovat was relieved to hear Group 1 firing on the battery, as he had not yet been able to contact Major Mills-

Roberts on his 18 Set. As Group 2 approached, the two assault troops separated onto separate routes to the north and south of Blancmesnl Wood. F Troop, on the northern axis, came under fire and were forced to screen their movement as they closed in on the battery with smoke. In the confusion, a 'blue on blue' fire-fight broke out, where F Troop engaged Colonel Lovat's HQ. However, as radio communication was now working well, the fire was checked before damage was done and was successfully redirected at the Germans, who were to be seen moving around, covered from Major Mills-Roberts's Group to the north of the battery.

COHQ reported in a public relations document that as F Troop cautiously closed in on the battery, they spotted a platoon of Germans debussing from a truck in a farmyard. In the confused situation, these troops, either the off-duty shift from the battery or a quick reaction force, were vulnerable and, as explained by Lord Lovat:

> 'There is no finer target at point-blank range than troops in or out of lorries before they have shaken into any fighting formation. They were liquidated, and we moved on to take up our final position.'

Meanwhile, B Troop was taking a less exposed route to the south of the wood, up a shallow valley that led to the battery's perimeter fence. Both troops reported to Commando HQ that they were in their assault positions. White phosphorous smoke grenades were prepared to cover the final advance to the enemy's wire, where Bangalore Torpedos were to be pushed under the pilled coils of dannert wire, to blow a route into the battery

At 0628 hours, just as Lord Lovat was preparing to fire the three white Verey lights that were to initiate the attack, another pair of Spitfires dived onto the battery, despite the fact that they were being pursued by German *Focke-Wulf* fighters. The cannon fire smashed into the battery, and inevitably, because the commandos were so close, they received some of the Spitfire's rounds. It is recorded by COHQ that two of Major Mills-Roberts's US Rangers, who were sniping at the Germans, 'were blown from the roof of a house, but were unhurt.' However, under the cover of Group 1's rapid small-arms fire and ten 3-inch mortar smoke rounds, the assault went in. Royal Artillery Officer Captain Porteous, with B Troop, recounted:

> 'Luckily, we found a spot on the wire... where obviously the German soldiers had been coming home late from leave or something

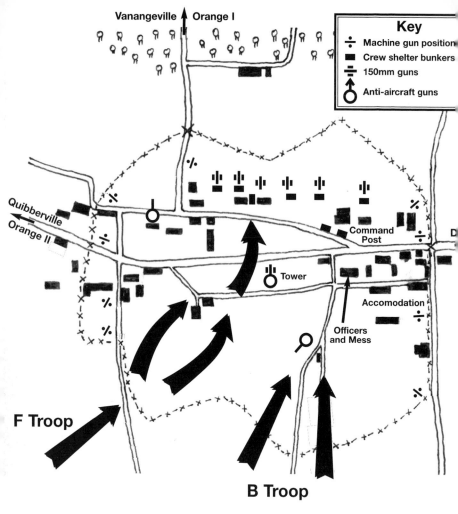

**Key**

- ÷ Machine gun position
- ■ Crew shelter bunkers
- ≡ 150mm guns
- ⚲ Anti-aircraft guns

Vanangeville  ↑ Orange I

Quibberville
Orange II

Command
Post

D

Tower

Accomodation

Officers
and Mess

**F Troop**

**B Troop**

*of the sort and had trampled a passage down through this bit of wire
at the back. We managed to get in without any problem at all. . . So
we then did a little bayonet charge into the gun pits themselves.'*

B Troop had benefited from a combination of luck, rare German
carelessness, and the increasingly desperate break-in battle that F
Troop were fighting just to their north. With about two hundred
yards of open ground to cover, F Troop were under heavy fire from
one of the 20mm flak guns and from riflemen deployed in the
centre of the battery position, firing from hedgerows and buildings
that had not been cleared from the site. The commandos of F Troop
started to suffer casualties, but Lord Lovat's men charged the
second belt of wire, which 'was crossed, in places, over the bodies
of our dead and wounded.' He went on to say, 'It was a stupendous

charge which went in, in many cases, over open ground swept by machine-gun fire.'

Major Pat Porteous, according to his Victoria Cross citation was

**The officers of F Troop wearing their own parent regiment's cap badges on their green berets.**

'In the initial assault . . . working with the smaller of the two detachments, was shot at close range through the hand, the bullet passing through his palm and entering his upper arm. Undaunted, Major Porteous closed with his assailant, succeeded in disarming him and killed him with his own bayonet, thereby saving the life of a British Sergeant on whom the German had turned his aim.'

Once inside the battery's perimeter, the sharp fight amongst the buildings and covered positions continued unabated. Sub-machine-gun fire and grenades were exchanged at close range as the commandos pushed on with determination. F Troop's Sergeant Major Stockdale's citation for the Distinguished Conduct Medal reads:

'Sergeant Major Stockdale took command of the troop after all his officers had been killed or had become casualties. TSM Stockdale, while leading a bayonet charge had part of his foot blown away by an enemy stick-bomb [sic]. Although in great pain, TSM Stockdale continued to engage the enemy. He set a splendid example and was an inspiration to his men.'

**Captain Pat Porteous VC.**

Stockdale had the satisfaction of limping around a building and felling the German grenadier with a burst from his Thompson sub-machine gun. Corporal Blunden received a well-deserved Military Medal for setting:

'...a high standard of leadership, and showed a great example in house-to-house, and hand-to-hand fighting through the battery buildings. He was wounded but refused to receive medical attention and continued to destroy the enemy until there were no Germans

**The ground across which the commandos attacked from the Blancmenil Wood to the centre of the battery.**

SW

B Troop

F Troop

Two barbed wire perimeter fences and mines

**Two of the Hesse Battery command post bunkers, now in the garden of a modern home. The gun pits lay beyond.**

*left alive.'*

Such was the ferocity of the fighting against German troops, whose quality and morale had not yet been sapped by events on the Russian front, to the extent that they were to be in 1944. However, at the Hess Battery, Lord Lovat explained that there was 'no pity for an enemy who knew no code and had no compassion'.

Despite the suppressive fire from Group 1. German machine-gun positions on the eastern flank of the large battery perimeter were still in action. Lovat recorded in his after-action report:

> *'Considerable numbers of Germans, who had hidden in underground tunnels containing stores and ammunition, in the battery office, under tables, in the cook house and out-buildings, were either bayoneted or shot at close range by sub-machine guns. Two officers including the military commander were also killed after a rousing chase from building to building.'*

Battery Commander *Hauptmann* Scholer was actually only wounded during the commando's clearance of his gun position. Armed only with a pistol, he fought well in the buildings in the centre of the battery, before finally being left for dead. By 0630 hours, fifteen minutes after Group 2 assaulted it, the battery was in Lord Lovat's hands.

Meanwhile, as B Troop, under cover of white phosphorous smoke from No. 77 Grenades, were completing the clearance of the battery in detail. F Troop had cleared the gun pits with grenades, and the commando engineers were at work preparing to blow the guns. They packed the specially prepared charges that they had carried in their Bergen rucksacks into the breaches of the six 150mm guns. With a shell ready in the gun barrel, the massive charges burst the barrels and blew off the breach blocks. So thorough were the demolitions, they even destroyed the gun sights to prevent their salvage. The official report records that 'at 0650 hours, five of the guns were blown up and shortly afterwards the sixth gun, which was a considerable distance away, was demolished alone by Lance Corporal Skerry.' In some cases, the commandos were only tens of yards away when the demolition charges exploded. Meanwhile, according to Major Mills-Roberts, 'a number of German snipers were now shooting up the battery area from outside.'

While No. 4 Commando was still in occupation of the battery, 'suddenly a squadron of *Messerschmitts* swept in low over the battery.' Major Mills-Roberts described the considerable presence of mind of the commandos:

> *'From the air, most troops looked alike, and so instead of taking cover, we waved genially to them, receiving in return a reassuring wave from the German Squadron Leader – their interference would have been an embarrassment. They were flying very low, but they did not tumble to the fact that we were not the rightful occupants of the battery.'*

The COHQ report recorded that with the guns destroyed and the battery searched for documents, 'before leaving the battery, the bodies of those who had fallen in the action were collected and laid down upon the site, after which the Union Jack was run up over the British dead.' With the Union flag flying, as a defiant calling-card on 813 *Batterie's* own officers' mess flagpole, No 4 Commando's withdrawal began at about 0700 hours.

## The Withdrawal

Lord Lovat always believed that the withdrawal was potentially the most difficult part of the operation, but he had carefully prepared for this phase. C Troop was holding a beachhead around

Landing craft waiting off Orange Beach I for the return of the commandos. Note the partly effective smoke screen.

Orange Beach 1, from which the whole Commando would be picked up by the waiting Royal Navy assault craft. He planned to avoid the more open Orange Beach 2, where he was certain that he would have been seen, in favour of the closer Orange 1. This was a sound plan as it later became apparent that German reinforcements had been waiting to ambush the commandos who they expected to return via Quiberville.

Not least of the problems of the withdrawal was the evacuation of the men wounded during the taking of the Hess Battery. The commandos would not leave the wounded to the Germans. As planned, a medical detachment came forward from Group 1 into the battery, and with the help of four German prisoners of war, evacuated the wounded on 'stretchers,' back through the woods towards Orange Beach 1. At least one of the stretchers was a door taken from a nearby building. One German gunner apparently protested that a medical officer had excused him from marching because of frostbite that he suffered on the Eastern Front, and that he should not be bearing stretchers. Captain Porteous had eventually collapsed from loss of blood and was one of the wounded to be carried back to the beachhead by the four German prisoners. He recalled that 'they needed a little encouragement with the bayonet and that the prisoners were also reluctant to approach the cliff top 'because they had laid all the mines there and they weren't quite sure where they were.'

Meanwhile, A Troop, which had been split between Group 1 and Group 2, were providing fighting patrols designed to dominate the area around the beachhead and the gap between Orange 1 and Orange 2. Just before they were due to withdraw, they spotted two five-man German patrols coming from the hamlet of St Marguerite, and identifying their route, Lieutenant Veasey deployed his men in hasty ambush position in the hedgerows. The commandos opened fire when the leading enemy infantrymen were just fifteen yards away. Several Germans fell, and the remainder beat a hasty retreat. Taking advantage of the enemy's confusion, Lieutenant Veasey led his section's withdrawal back to Orange 1 'with all possible speed.' An old French lady, who had witnessed the action, apparently gave an egg to each of the commandos as they passed.

As Lord Lovat ordered the withdrawal from the battery, the volume of enemy small-arms and mortar fire increased, but it was inaccurate and sporadic. The longer the commandos remained at the battery, the more coordinated the German response would become. However, the Germans had now realised roughly where the commando's re-embarkation would take place, and unobserved 81mm medium mortar fire targeted the area of the gully and Orange 1 Beach. In reply, the commandos' own 3-inch medium mortar concentrated on keeping the German infantry at bay with high explosive rounds while the 2-inch Mortar Section fired smoke. With A Troop already climbing down the cliff and embarking, B Troop, followed by F Troop, passed through C Troop into the tight cliff-top beachhead.

Once the assault force were within the perimeter of the beachhead and were scrambling down the gully, C Troop started what was potentially the most difficult part of the withdrawal. They had to finally break clean from the enemy and escape across the beach to the landing craft. At 0815 hours they began a manoeuvre that they had repeatedly practised during training, in which Bren guns, working in pairs, withdrew alternately behind the 2-inch mortar smoke screen. The fire and manoeuvre worked well, and smoke was used liberally to obscure the commandos, who were dashing from cover to cover.

During the landing, each commando from Group 1 had carried two No. 18 Smoke

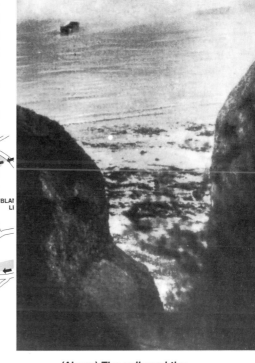

(Above) The gully and the landing craft waiting off Orange I Beach.

(left) The area of Orange used for the withdrawal of both Group 1 and 2.

**No. 4 Commando leaving behind the smoke shrouded Vasterville cliffs overlooking Orange I Beach.**

Generators up the gully, and dumped them at the top of the gully for use during the final stages of the withdrawal. Similar devices shrouded the beach with billowing clouds, and to cover the waiting LCAs, the Royal Navy set off smoke floats, and the Germans fired blindly into the resulting grey clouds. The COHQ report described the re-embarkation of No. 4 Commando:

> 'The re-embarkation began at 0730 hours, three extra LCAs being sent from the Boat Pool to assist. During the re-embarkation, shells burst about every half-minute on the beach, some 500 yards to the Westward, causing no casualties. The exceeding flatness of the beach and the fast-ebbing tide made re-embarkation difficult. The LCAs were taken in as far as was deemed practicable and the troops then waded out to them, sometimes up to their necks. Throughout this operation, the Goatley collapsible boat, which had been landed by the second flight, proved useful in ferrying the wounded. She was paddled by a short red-faced Commando Trooper clad solely in a "Mae West" and a woollen cap. The Boat Officers of the LCAs displayed sound seamanship in coping with their task. Smoke was extensively used, the Mark VI Smoke-floats being very effective.'

The final men of C Troop waded out to the LCAs, and fell exhausted into the bottom of the landing craft. No. 4 Commando had made good its escape. But once out of the smoke's cover, and as they motored into view of enemy positions further along the cliff, they came under fire again. As they withdrew, the commandos returned rifle and machine-gun fire with the German infantry around the lighthouse.

The relief after battle begins to show among Lovat's men on the passage back to England.

No. 4 Commando's return to Newhaven on the morning of 20 August 1942.

On the passage home to Newhaven, the commandos had time to reflect on their success, lucky escapes, and those who had lost their lives in the operation. They picked up an RAF pilot who landed in his parachute virtually alongside one of the craft, and another two pilots were picked up from the motor launch marking the swept channel through the minefield.

The casualties suffered by No. 4 Commando were five officers and forty-one Other Ranks, of whom two officers and nine ORs had been killed and thirteen men were listed as missing. This was not an inconsiderable proportion of the 265 men who landed two hours and forty minutes earlier.

The raid on the Hess Battery had been a success. As with all elements of the Jubilee Force, the commandos were well trained, but their part in the operation was based on sound intelligence information. In addition Lord Lovat and his men of No 4 Commando not only had a good plan but also good fortune on their side. COHQ reported that 'this hazardous assault on "Hess" Battery was carried out strictly according to plan and may well become a model for future operations of this kind.'

**US Ranger Sergeant Sizma lighting a celebratory cigarette back in Newhaven.**

# CHAPTER SIX

# INNER FLANK ATTACK I: BLUE BEACH – PUYS

In addition to the commandos' destruction of the flanking Hess and Goebbels batteries, a part of the Jubilee plan was to land two Canadian battalions on what was termed the Inner Flanks: Blue and Green Beaches. These beaches were respectively a mile to the east and west of the main frontal assault on Dieppe. The aim of the Inner Flank attacks were to clear the eastern and western headlands and to extend the raid's frontage, thus dissipating the German force. In addition, Green Beach was to be a beachhead from which a further battalion, was to attack the German airfield to the south-west of Dieppe. Both landing grounds were relatively small beaches in the wall of cliffs to the east and west of Dieppe, where the villages of Puys (Blue Beach) and Pourville (Green Beach) had been fashionable resorts, with substantial hotels and villas.

The two assault battalions would attack at the same time as the commandos, at 0450 hours, which was half an hour after the beginning of nautical twilight, with a predicted visibility of just two hundred years. By deciding on this time, the Canadians' approach to their two beaches would be under the cover of darkness in order to achieve 'a sufficient measure of surprise'. The Combined Ops report goes onto explain, 'It was essential for the plan that the Royal

*Blue Beach intelligence photos*

**(Above left) View from the beach towards the eastern cliffs and the White House.**

**(Above right) The view to the beach from the eastern cliffs over the White House.**

**(left) The beach, seawall and the slope up which the Canadians would have to attack.**

Regiment of Canada should touch down exactly at Zero hour, 0450 hours...'

There was to be no naval gunfire support before or during the landing. As with the commandos, the Inner Flank attacks relied totally on surprise to get ashore in what was hoped would be 'a largely unopposed landing'. The main landing at Dieppe would take place thirty minutes later at 0520 hours.

### Blue Beach and the Plan

The orders for Blue Beach, given verbally to Lieutenant Colonel Catto were as follows:

*'The Royal Regiment of Canada will land on Blue Beach and secure the headland east of Jubilee [Dieppe] with a minimum of delay. There you will destroy the local objectives, which consist of machine-gun posts, heavy and light flak installations and a 4-gun howitzer battery south and east of the town. The battalion will then come into reserve and detach a company to protect an engineer demolition party operating in the gasworks and power plant.'*

The beach that the Royals were to fight over was described to the Commanding Officer as being a narrow shingle beach with a tall sea wall at its rear. Beyond the wall, there was the small village of Puys and a steep valley running inland. Maps and accompanying air photographs were useful but most information was gleaned, in the best traditions of intelligence, from pre war tourist photographs and postcards, which had been assiduously collected from families across Britain. The Canadian infantrymen produced comprehensive description of the main obstacle that they would face from these sources.

*'This [the sea] wall is made of masonry and is about 100 yards long with a vertical face ten to twelve feet high, with two flights of steps leading to its top, one about half-way down its length and the other at the south-west end. It runs just above the high-water line along the beach which is 250 yards long and 300 yards wide. The beach has two exits; a footpath at the north-east end and a road moving straight inland up a small valley to the village of Puys.'*

In the event, the Royals found the sea wall 'covered with heavy wire, and on the landward side was a deep and very thick obstacle of tangled wire'.

However, little was known about the enemy and the number of Germans that would be encountered but les Glycines Holiday Camp was known to be used as a small barracks. In addition, as indicated by the mission given above, photo interpreters had spotted a number of enemy positions that were marked on the overprinted intelligence map. These were mainly sandbagged field fortifications but what intelligence had not spotted was a concrete pillbox in the garden of the 'White House', which was carefully camouflaged and sited to cover the beach. Other skilfully sited positions, built into buildings and into the sea wall to the west of the beach, were also unidentified.

The Germans of 12 *Kompanie*, III/Battalion, 571 *Infanterie* Regiment held the area of the Eastern Headland and the village of Puys. A platoon of about forty men held the beach defences, covering the shingle of Blue Beach. Other platoon positions on the Eastern Headland could also cover the seaward approaches and parts of the Puys beach.

Lieutenant Colonel Catto's plan was for A Company to tackle the sea wall and clear Puys. C Company was to deal with light anti-aircraft guns on the 150-foot high Eastern or le Polet headland, which had two prominent landmarks; a Church steeple and a semaphore station. A Company would then clear the area of the holiday camp and one platoon of this company would go on to

**The intelligence overprint showing the defences east of Dieppe and around Blue Beach at Puys.**

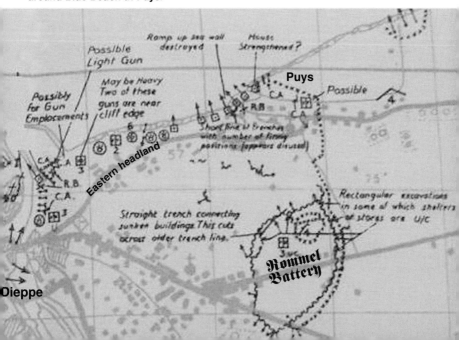

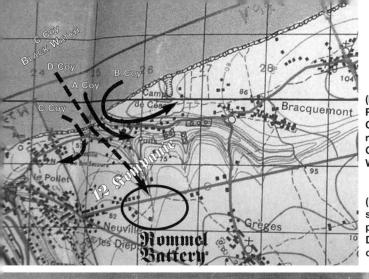

(Left) The Royal Regiment of Canada's plan, with reinforcement by C Company of Black Watch.

(Below) One of a series of air photographs of the Dieppe area taken on 30 June 1942.

attack and clear a machine-gun posts in this area. It was vital for Jubilee's success that the headland should be in Canadian hands when the main landing started thirty minutes after the Royals touched down. On the Battalion's left B Company would deal with a heavy anti-aircraft battery near the edge of the cliff, then capture some light anti-aircraft guns in the same area and mop up German marines in the coastguard houses on the cliff further to the west.

The second wave of Battalion Headquarters and D Company of the Royals were to be followed by a third wave, consisting of the Mortar Platoon and C Company Black Watch of Canada, who were to attack an enemy defended location south of the village of Puys. This consisted of an emplaced four-gun battery (Code named Rommel), anti-aircraft guns and machine guns. The Royals would subsequently establish contact with the Essex Scottish, who would be landing on the main Dieppe Beach. If time allowed, the Royal Regiment of Canada was to seize the gasworks, and, as mentioned in their orders, protect an engineer demolition party. Thereafter, the Royals would become brigade reserve, while the Black Watch and the accompanying Royal Canadian Artillery field and anti-aircraft gunners, would man any enemy guns captured intact on the Eastern Headland and use them against another German battery further inland. The gunners were also to bring back parts of what were thought to be a new patterns of German guns.

### The Assault

The five hundred and fifty men of the Royals sailed from Portsmouth, split between three Landing Ships Infantry, the *Queen Emma*, *Princess Astrid* and the *Duke of Wellington*, escorted by a pair

**The Portsmouth part of the Dieppe flotilla at sea on the evening of 18 August**

of gunboats. Reporter Ross Munro wrote:

> *'The officers and men had been told by now that they were going to Dieppe tonight and there were hurried conferences aboard the ship, refresher briefings and eleventh-hour preparations. Few of the Royals seemed to be as confident a mood as I had known them in the "Practice Dieppe" [Yukon]. The rush to the port and the mass of details, which had to be crammed again in a few hours left everyone rather ragged.'*

Their crossing went to plan and at 0258 hours, the Landing Craft Assault were lowered from the mother ships' davits. However, there was some confusion and a delay of twenty all too vital minutes, when the LCAs mistakenly formed up on a motor gunboat from another group. Order restored but badly delayed the Royals were ready to head for the beach.

> *'The passage to the beach was controlled by . . . Lieutenant Commander Goulding. He brought the Flotilla in on a course South by 5 [degrees] West, which enabled him to sight Dieppe and then to alter course to the eastward so as to pick up the valley behind "Blue Beach", a spot very narrow and difficult to identify. As the flotilla was passing the piers of Dieppe, the harbour lights were put on and recognition signals flashed in Morse Code. . . As the Royal Regiment of Canada came in, searchlights began to play over the sea for as long a period as an hour, according to the estimate of a survivor.'*

Even though they caught up some time on the run in to the beach the delay in forming up meant that the Royals landed seventeen minutes late, at 0507 hours, when it was already getting light. In the growing daylight the essential tactical surprise was lost and as one officer commented, 'the enemy was ready and waiting and would have had to be asleep to miss us'.

Corporal Ellis of A Company reported ...that objects could clearly be distinguished while the craft were still half a mile from the beach and were under observation and under fire before they

A German snap shot of infantry positions on the cliffs flanking Pu

landed. The enemy's plunging small arms fire from the cliff top negated much of the protection afforded by the lightly armoured sides of the LCA. The Royals were consequently suffering casualties, including Battalion Second-in-Command, Major Scholfield, before landing. However, German fire intensified as soon as the first wave of landing craft began to touchdown. Lieutenant Commander Goulding wrote 'In several cases officers and men were killed or wounded on the ramp as they made to leave the boats'. The COHQ report recorded:

> 'It was seen to be coming principally from a white houses on the left and from pillboxes on the cliff firing straight down into the craft. Most of the officers, all of whom led their men with great gallantry, were killed or wounded immediately.'

Lieutenant Walter Hopener, commanding 12 *Kompanie*, 571 *Infanterie* Regiment was in a bunker over looking Blue Beach:

> 'As the landing ramps fell and the attackers sprang firing onto land, they met the destructive fire of the two heavy MGs. An inferno began which was to last almost three hours. In our command post, two young soldiers who had only been here a few days threw up constantly – it was their first action.
>
> 'We were amazed at the attacker, who fought with bravery and élan against an opponent who could not be seen. Nobody thought of giving up. Taking effective cover behind their dead comrades, they shot uninterruptedly at our positions. Thus with their bodies these dead soldiers provided their comrades with the last service of friendship.'

From the German command post instructions were passed to their artillery for defensive fire tasks. Captain Browne, the artillery Forward Observation Officer attached to the Royals wrote of the enemy battery's response to the landing:

> 'The defensive fire of the German artillery (as I was later told by a German soldier, 75 mm infantry guns) was extremely well surveyed, for the shells burst precisely at the water-line at impeccably correct intervals of timing. I saw two LCAs sunk by hits or splinters from this fire. From a gunners point of view this was admirable shooting.'

However, machine guns were causing most of the casualties. Private Creer of A Company, who were attempting to attack Puys over the sea wall, recalled in his debriefing that 'There was a big house just back from the wall, and there seemed to be a machine gun firing from every window'. Similar fire positions in another house on the left flank enfiladed the beach. Corporal Ellis commented:

> 'The beach was... plainly visible to the Germans, whose own fire positions were extraordinarily well concealed from our view. The Royals were shot down in heaps on the beach without knowing where the fire was coming from.'

Under heavy fire, the Royals attempted to cross the sea wall but as the COHQ report states that the Canadians were '... forced into a state of inaction, having lost heavily on crossing the beach... and still more heavily when they reached the sea-wall, about fifty yards from the water's edge'. There were also a number of well concealed machine-gun posts built into the sea wall itself, of which the Royals had been unaware. The official historian wrote that 'Courageous efforts were made by officers and men of the first wave to cut or blow passages through the wire obstacles on the wall and reach the enemy positions'. At least one Bangalore Torpedo was thrust under the wire and successfully blown on the eastern part of the beach by

Captain Sinclair and Corporal Ellis. At this stage, the number of Canadians forcing their way through the gap in the wire was too few to overcome enemy resistance. Amongst those moving in-land were Captain Sinclair, who fell wounded, and Corporal Ellis who pressed on alone up the hill towards one of the buildings. Finding the building unoccupied, he spotted an enemy position and successfully engaged the occupants who were

**The point where the Royals crossed the seawall at the left hand end of the beach.**

Pillbox

White House

Pillbox

manning a *Spandau*. Meanwhile, back on the beach, some of the machine gun posts built into the sea wall itself were knocked out at a heavy cost. Captain Browne described the clearance of one of enemy positions by Lieutenant Wedd:

> *'Leaving the LCA at touchdown with his platoon, he reached the wall with little more than a section, and there found he was still being fired upon by one of the wall posts, a pillbox. There being apparently no other way of attacking the weapon, he left his corner of relative shelter and sprinted the short distance directly toward the pill-box with a No. 36 grenade. With complete disregard for his own*

Pillboxes

safety, and displaying great skill, he flung the grenade through the fire slit of the pillbox, killing all its occupants and putting the gun out of action. His body, riddled with bullets, was later picked up in front of the pillbox.'

The Combined Ops report recorded that 'A and B Companies were dwindling away to nothing...' To make matters worse, the naval gunfire support of HMS *Garth*, who had come into action in support of the Royals at 0520 hours, unlike the low velocity weapons mounted on gunboats at Orange and Yellow Beaches, was doing little to help the Canadians. Unsuppressed enemy batteries were forcing her to remain at a safe distance out to sea under cover

**A ship's Royal Navy and Royal Marines gun crew in action.**

of the smoke screen. In these conditions, the destroyer was unable to keep the cliff top to the right of the beach under continuous bombardment. Lieutenant Commander Scatchard reported:

'It was a matter of going in through the smoke till close, squaring off [to fire] and then retiring, then circling round and repeating the manoeuvre. On each occasion, we were straddled and it seems extraordinary that more ships were not hit.

'He [Captain Browne] called for fire at a white house on the cliff top, which we answered, but I regret did not hit. He was not in a position to spot [fall of shot] and all we could see were the rounds falling short and hitting the cliff face.'

118

It is worth recording at this point that one of the recommendations resulting from Operation Jubilee was that ships tasked to support land forces 'should have bombardment charges'. The Hunt Class destroyers at Dieppe held in their magazines high velocity, low trajectory, Semi Armour Piercing (SAP) rounds that were designed for use in ship to ship engagements. For bombarding the coast, a lower velocity high trajectory round was required that could be lobbed inland. With the wrong type of charges *Garth* and the other destroyers would be lucky to hit a target on the cliff top.

**The Second and Third Wave**

The landing craft carrying Lieutenant Colonel Catto's headquarters, along with C and D Companies landed approximately twenty minutes late, at 0530 hours, having sailed well to the west as a result of a navigational error. As the Royals' second wave started their run-in, the Boston Day Bombers hit the cliff top to the right of the beach with a mixed load of HE and smoke. However, by the time the second wave reached the beach 'the smoke laid by the RAF had almost entirely disappeared, traces only remained in the treetops above the beach'.

The second wave landed on the right flank of the beach but, as described by Ross Munro in a newspaper article, they came under heavy fire:

> *'Vicious bursts of yellow tracer from German machine guns made a veritable curtain around the craft... As soon as the ramp at the bow of our boat fell, fifteen Royals rushed the beach and sprinted up the slope, taking cover along the cliff side. Machine gun fire held back the rest...'*

What Munro could not mention in a wartime newspaper column was that there were many casualties and both landing craft and beach were now littered with further crumpled khaki bodies. In a post war book he described the 'nightmare of the blood stained beach at Puys'.

> *'There was one young lad crouching six feet away from me in the LCA. He had made several vain attempts to rush down the ramp to the beach but each time a hail of fire had driven him back. He had been wounded in the arm but was determined to try again. He lunged forward and a streak of red-white tracer slashed through his stomach.*
>
> *'I'll never forget his anguished cry as he collapsed on the blood-soaked deck: "Christ, we gotta beat them; we gotta beat them!" He*

119

*was dead in a few minutes.'*

*'Canadians were running [east] along the bottom of the cliff towards the stone wall. They carried their weapons and some were firing as they ran. But some had no helmets, some were already wounded, their uniforms torn and bloody. One by one they were cut down and rolled down the shingle slope to the sea.*

*'On no other front have I witnessed such carnage. It was brutal; and terrible and shocked you to insensibility to see the piles of dead and feel the hopelessness of the attack at this point.'*

The four craft carrying the third wave, consisting of the Royals' Mortar Platoon and the attached Black Watch company, landed under the cliff to the west of the sea wall at 0545 hours. Colonel Stacey described the situation that faced them:

*'Here the main body of survivors of the waves landed earlier were gathered; they had set up Bren guns among the rocks and were firing at the house on the right hand cliff, which was still spouting fire. Lt Koyl, however, said that "Germans were visible on the west cliff also and were engaged by the naval craft with Lewis guns".'*

The surviving Canadian infantry were reported to be:

*'To the westward side of the Beach up against the base of the cliffs, the main body of the first landing of troops were heavily engaged firing up to the enemy on the cliff top also against enemy positions in houses halfway up the cliffs to the east.'*

Little is known of the fate of the soldiers of C Company the Black Watch, as the only men who returned were those who had been wounded in or near the landing craft. It is assumed that the soldiers of this company were virtually all killed or wounded on the fire swept beach. If any of the accompanying Royals' 3-inch mortars,

**The western end of the seawall and the slope up to the houses of Puys. One of the points where a few of the Royals got off the beach.**

Dieppe →

SEA WALL

A and B
Companies

Bn HQ

0530   C and D
Companies

0545   BLACK WATCH

who were also in the third wave, came into action, they only fired a handful of rounds before the crews were also hit.

Despite the dire situation, with grenades being thrown down the cliff, the Canadians were determined to get off Blue Beach. Some time after 0610 hours, Lieutenant Colonel Catto and a small party of officers and men of the Royals and the Royal Canadian Artillery, including Captain Browne 'got off the beach by cutting a path through the wire at the western end of the sea wall'. According to Captain Browne's report there were:

**A German infantryman photographed on the cliffs of Dieppe.**

'*No Bangalore torpedoes available here, as those allotted to D Company had been lost overside from the LCA which carried them, and C Company's Bangalore men had been shot down as they landed. In these circumstances, the only means of getting through the wire was the use of wire-cutters. The Colonel, Sergeant Coles and two other ranks finally cut a path and through this passage went a party consisting of six officers and fifteen other ranks. . .*

'*I left my telegraphist, who was in the middle of a message, with his 66 set on the beach, telling him to follow later; but neither he nor anyone else was able to follow us . . . because machine gun fire from a new position immediately came down on the gap in the wire.*'

Consequently, at 0700 hours, Colonel Catto's small party was cut off from the remainder of C and D Companies on the beach. However, reaching the top of the cliff above the western end of the sea wall, the party cleared two large buildings with little resistance. Captain Browne describes the situation as a whole:

'*Sounds of firing on the left flank had now died completely away. From the centre and the right flank, we could hear intermittent bursts of German automatic fire and the steady detonations of their mortar bombs. From this we inferred that A and B Companies had been knocked out, and that the survivors of C and D Companies were still pinned down in the angle of the cliff, being cut up by mortars. We discovered that we could not get back to the beach, nor could we get back to the cliff edge because of LMG fire from the left*

**Wehrmacht** infantry machine gunners and mortar crew advancing on the cliffs of Dieppe.

*flank, up on the hillside.'*

Seeing a strong group of German infantry advancing from the direction of enemy positions in the centre of the beach, presumably released from their task of containing the now destroyed or neutralized A and B Companies, Lieutenant Colonel Catto's party withdrew westward along the cliff towards Dieppe in the hope of making contact with the Essex Scottish. They got away and reached the main road running between Puys and Dieppe where they eventually went to ground in a wood to the east of an 88 mm anti-aircraft battery that was one of the Royals' objectives. From the cover of woods Colonel Catto's party watched the battery in action. Captain Browne wrote:

> *The 88-mm Battery of 6 guns on the cliff top... served its guns magnificently. It was low-level-bombed at least four times and machine gunned often by our fighters after 1000 hrs, that is, between 1000 hrs and 1600 hrs, with us as witnesses, and each time the guns were back in action within a matter of a few seconds, firing upon the departing aircraft. Once, after a low-level attack, only two guns were instantly back in action, the other times always at least four.'*

Back on Blue Beach there were further futile attempts to scale the cliffs to escape the withering cross fire on the beach. Gunner Rowe recorded:

> *'... a corporal organized a small party to attempt to get up the cliff. As soon as they came into the open three were killed and I was wounded... I saw a captain and a party try to scale the cliff. All of*

*the party were knocked out and the captain alone got half way up the
cliff and then his body came rolling down.'*

## The Attempted Withdrawal

Radio communication with the Royal Canadians on Blue Beach was
poor. This was partly the result of the Battalion HQ Number 18 set
getting wet during the landing and the battalion, consequently,
relied on Captain Browne's No. 66 set, which was designed to
communicate with the Royal Navy's ships. In this case, HMS *Garth*
was very slow in passing his situation reports on to the HQ ship
HMS *Calpe*. Other radio users passed a series of contradictory
messages before going off the air. This further confused the
situation rather than adding clarity. As a result, General Roberts
never developed a clear picture of what was going on on Blue
Beach. He even tasked air reconnaissance to try to establish what
was happening. However, what was eventually clear was that from
about 0630 hours, repeated requests for evacuation from the beach
were received by landing craft, mother and HQ ships.

The attempted evacuation of the Royals consisted of numerous
attempts by landing craft to close on the beach to pick up surviving
Canadian infantrymen. The following examples are typical of the
efforts made by the Royal Navy to get the Canadians off the beach.
Lieutenant Ramsey commander of LCA 209 headed inshore some
time between 0600 and 0700 hours. The Flotilla Officer of the *Queen
Emma* recorded that:

*'... a radio message was sent out from Blue Beach asking all
LCAs to return to the beach to evacuate the beach party... LCA 209,
went in under covering fire of an LCS [Landing Craft Support].
Upon reaching the beach, the boat was swamped with soldiers and
forced to retire. Very heavy fire was encountered and many of the
soldiers were killed or wounded. Owing to the jam and excess of
personnel in the boat, it was impossible for the doors to be housed
up, and a fair amount of water was shipped. When the craft was
about 50 yards from the beach, she was hit by a heavy gun and
capsized.'*

Private Simpson was amongst the infantrymen on the beach
watching the LCA approach:

*'... and orders were given to board her. There was a terrible
scramble and nearly everyone (still alive) made for the small ramp
doors. The slaughter was awful. The boat had to be pushed off the
beach. It was so full of holes it began to sink. At that time, I would*

*venture to say at least fifty men were aboard. Bullets were still pouring in and a bomb landed alongside. It turned over on its keel and stayed afloat. A few men swam away, while others and myself clung to the still floating craft. We were only about a hundred yards from the shore and were still being blasted by enemy fire. From what I saw, there was no life on the beach.'*

Only a handful of men either swam from the wrecks to safety or were picked up by other landing craft that braved the enemy fire. Without the effective support of a destroyer attempts to rescue the Royals went on until mid morning, at the cost of mounting naval casualties.

Eventually, with grenades being 'lobbed down from the cliff top above' and machine gun fire emanating from 'inaccessible German positions', the remaining survivors of the three companies stranded on the western end of the beach surrendered at about 0800 hours. It is probable that by this time over half of the men were dead and of the remainder, few can have been unwounded. Gunner Rowe who was clinging to an overturned LCA just off the beach recorded that 'After all the firing had died down, the Germans came down with stretchers and started clearing the beaches'. Those on the beach recalled that the nervous defenders shouted at them in German:

**The German evacuate the wounded Royals from the beach.**

**The ubiquitous German photographer captures the Royal's surrender.**

> '... until several English speakers yelled, "Put your hands on top of your head. Quickly now, or you will be shot." We could see that they would not take no for an answer. We climbed up one of the cliff ladders passed the piled bodies of the rest of the battalion who had died trying to force a passage though the wire.'

Meanwhile, Captain Browne and the rest of Lieutenant Colonel Catto's party, lying up in the wood south of the Eastern Headland, heard the Germans marching the prisoners away from the beach shortly after 1000 hours. This group, without chance of escape, though concealed from German reinforcements on the roads and in the fields around them, saw little military value in their situation and surrendered during the course of the afternoon. The Royal Regiment of Canada had all but ceased to exist.

Of the 554 Royals who set out on Operation Jubilee, only two officers and sixty-two Other Ranks, most of whom were wounded

**225 dead Royals were gathered on Blue Beach by the Germans.**

to some extent, returned to England. The Royals suffered more heavily than any other Canadian battalion at Dieppe. To this total must be added the loss of seventy men of the Black Watch of Canada. The inner flank landing at Blue Beach had been a disaster and according to Ross Munro, 'Nobody had counted on casualties like this'. The whole plan had relied on surprise but the landing was late and made in full daylight. To compound matters, the enemy on the headlands had not been suppressed by bombing or naval bombardment and once the landing force were in trouble the Royal Navy's Hunt Class destroyers were unable to provide adequate assistance.

**The dead lay on the beach waiting to be collected by the victors.**

CHAPTER SEVEN

# INNER FLANK ATTACK II: GREEN BEACH

On the western Inner Flank, the South Saskatchewan Regiment (SSR) were to land on the beach at the small but popular holiday resort of Pourville, a mile and a half west of the main Dieppe landings, and three miles east of the Orange beaches and No. 4 Commando. As with the other flank attacks, the time of the landing on Green Beach was 0450 hours.

The Pourville beach (Green Beach) is overlooked by cliffs to the east and the west. Immediately behind the beach is an eight-foot-high sea wall. Though by no means as formidable as the wall at Blue Beach, with plenty of barbed wire it was still a significant obstacle – especially if the enemy were alert. Beyond it lay the village of Pourville, on 'what is in effect a narrow strip of land between the marshy flats of the Scie and the sea.' To make the river Scie valley more of an obstacle, the Germans had inundated much of the valley bottom, thus extending these marshy flats almost to the sea wall.

The Germans who were holding the coastline from the western end of the Dieppe Esplanade to Pourville were 8 *Kompanie* II/571 *Infantarie* Regiment. Their efforts were divided between manning positions overlooking Dieppe itself and the cliffs west of Pourville, while a platoon of about forty men were positioned in Pourville

**Looking west from the Western Headland across Green Beach, Pourville and the Scie Valley to a further set of cliffs.**

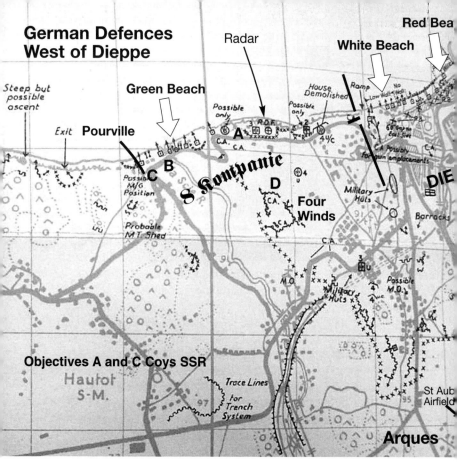

German Defences West of Dieppe

Radar

Red Bea

White Beach

Steep but possible ascent

Green Beach

House Demolished

Ramp

Exit  Pourville

Possible only

Possible only

3 R.D.F.

A

C.A.  C.A.

4/c

C  B

8 Kompanie

Possib M/G Position

D

⊕4

C.A.

Four Winds

Military Huts

DIE

Barracks

Probable M.T. Shed

M.O.

Military Huts

Possible M.O.

C.A.

Objectives A and C Coys SSR

Hautot S-M.

Trace Lines for Trench System

97

St Aub Airfield

95

Arques

covering Green Beach and the Scie Valley. As elsewhere on the Dieppe coast, the Germans had fully exploited the defensive qualities of the terrain, and had strongly fortified the high ground that afforded good fields of fire across both the beach and the valley. In the centre of the headland east of the beach stood one of the chain of German radar (RDF) stations that kept watch on the coast, along with a couple of anti-aircraft batteries, one of which was in the process of building protective concrete casemates at the time of the raid.

The South Saskatchewan Regiment, commanded by Lieutenant Colonel Merrit, was to land astride the River Scie and establish a beachhead 'with the minimum delay to enable the Queen's Own Cameron Highlanders of Canada to pass through without opposition' and attack the enemy airfield south of Dieppe. The Camerons were to meet up with the tanks of the Calgary Regiment, which would be landing on the main beach at Dieppe and attack

F

The inundated Scie Valley and the high ground east of Poutville, photographed during February 1942.

the reported divisional headquarters location in the château of Arques-la-Bataille. Meanwhile, the South Saskatchewans had the task of clearing the usual collection of gun positions between Green Beach and Dieppe.

The inundation of the valley behind the beach shaped the detail of Colonel Merrit's plan, but as there was sufficient space on the beach, all four companies were to land in a single wave. A Company on the left (east) flank:

> '...would immediately operate against the high ground to the east of Pourville capturing two light anti-aircraft guns, as well as the RDF station on the cliff and other guns nearby. This company would subsequently consolidate, make contact with the Royal Hamilton Light Infantry [RHLI, who were to land on the main beach].'

D Company, landing in the centre left, would clear Pourville east of the Scie bridge and strike inland in a south-easterly direction to clear and to take a battery that was described in briefings as being light, but marked on the intelligence overprint as being heavy. Then having linked up with the RHLI, they were to secure 'les 4 Vents Farm' or as it was known to the Canadians, 'Four Winds Farm.'

According to Colonel Stacey, C Company on the battalion's right, were ordered to clear 'a large white hotel overlooking the beach. This building turned out to be the quarters of a group of foreigners [slave or forced labour], some of which at least were Belgian'. C Company was then to take and hold the headland to the west of the beach until the Cameron Highlanders had advanced up

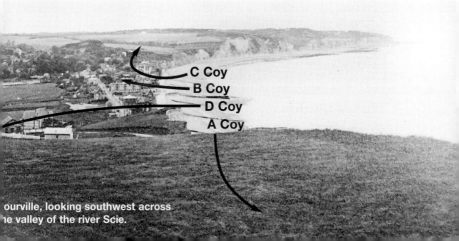

C Coy
B Coy
D Coy
A Coy

ourville, looking southwest across
ie valley of the river Scie.

**(Above)** The 'large white hotel' used by the Germans, now distincly grey.

**(Left)** A winter photograph of Pourville West.

the Scie Valley *en route* to their tasks at the airfield and the German headquarters. In the right centre, B Company was to clear Pourville, west of the Scie, including a building thought to be a German officers' mess, and take an infantry defensive position a little way inland. The Saskatchewans would subsequently form the western portion of the temporary defensive perimeter around Dieppe. It was planned that the battalion's eventual withdrawal would be via the main beach at Dieppe.

### The RDF Question

As has already been described, the examination and recovery of parts of the German RDF site on the cliffs above Dieppe had not

**A later verion of the Giant Wurtzburg radar hit by Allied bombing.**

been one of the original aims of the Operation. However, on hearing about the planned raid, the Air Ministry requested that it be included in the list of objectives. Flight Sergeant Cox, who had seized components from a Wurzburg radar during the Bruneval Raid, had in many respects provided as many questions as answers about German RDF capabilities. Of particular interest were questions such as, how would the longer-range, wide-beam radar, code-named Freyer, work alongside the Wurtzburg, and did the set have an anti-jamming capability? Answers to these and other questions were needed if the Allies were to successfully pursue this aspect of the technological war. After all, it was Churchill who wrote in a Cabinet minute:

> *'This war is not, however, a war of masses of men hurling masses of shells at each other. It is by devising new weapons and above all by scientific leadership that we shall best cope with the enemy's superior strength.'*

Defining the enemy's radar capability thought the capture of

**The RDF site was on the cliff to the east of Pourville.**

RDF

componants was difficult for, since Bruneval, as the Germans had considerably strengthened the defences around RDF sites. Thus a raid by a major landing force was a heaven-sent opportunity for the British radar scientists; Freya Radar Number 28 and its operators from 23 *Funkmess Kompanie* were in the area to be temporarily seized by the Canadians. To send a scientist was too much of a risk because although he would be able to find out much about the German technology just by looking at a set, if captured, many British secrets might be revealed. So, as before, an RAF radar technician rather than a scientist would be chosen for the task. Even so, there was a considerable risk of compromising British capabilities. The orders given to the South Saskatchewan Regiment instructed them '...to provide adequate protection, as the RDF expert must under no circumstances fall into enemy hands.' Whether these orders meant killing the expert has been debated over the years, but the dozen Canadians of the 'Special Platoon' attached to A Company, who were to escort Flight Sergeant Nissenthall, certainly thought so.

Freyer Radar.

Nissenthall briefed the platoon:

*'If we get into the RDF station, we may want to carry some equipment away. It will be heavy and possibly fragile. The valves – tubes to you – could be as big as a Chinese vase, and about as delicate.'*

The Freyer's antenna was a tall lattice affair, but the majority of the station, a solid concrete blockhouse, was below ground level, with several feet of packed earth providing extra protection from bombs. At 0345 hours on the morning of 19 August 1942, the duty Freya operator staring at his screen deep in this bunker, spotted the five columns of the Jubilee naval force off the coast. He called his site commander, Lieutenant Willi Webber, who having decided that these were not false echoes, contacted the Navy HQ, who dismissed the radar echoes as being the expected convoy of five ships. Webber replied:

*'I can only repeat that these are not five simple ships, but five columns of vessels. With respect, this cannot be a small convoy coming from Boulogne. If they were, they would appear from the east. These are coming from the north.'*

The German naval officer may have disregarded the warning, but the army watchkeepers, who Webber rang next, were far more receptive. Some time after 0400 hours, the Germans started the

The No. 3 Rifle, Sten gun, their ammuntion and grenades all needed checking and adjusting before battle.

process of alerting the defenders along the Dieppe coast.

### The Crossing and Landing

The South Saskatchewan Regiment embarked on their LSIs at Southampton, the *Princess Beatrix* and *Invicta*. In the cramped spaces below decks, the soldiers of the South Saskatchewan carried out their battle preparation. New weapons were prepared and ammunition distributed. Among the ammunition was an allocation of two No. 36 Grenades per man, plus reserves held at company and battalion level in the hands, respectively, of the company sergeant majors and the Regimental Sergeant Major. The grenades had to be cleaned of protective grease and wax before use. At about 2300 hours, the men of C Company

A prewar photograph of Pourville, looking south-west along the beach.

Germans laying mines and barbed wire.

aboard *Invicta* were going through the routine of cleaning and fusing their hand grenades when one of the bombs exploded. Seventeen soldiers were wounded. Not a good start; and with battle preparations and pre-battle nerves, few of the South Saskatchewans were able to get much sleep.

As scheduled, just before 0300 hours, with the mother ships at anchor, the men clambered down into their ten LCAs and two Landing Craft Mechanical (LCM). Without any confusion, the landing craft followed their gunboat escorts towards Green Beach; and without any apparent navigational errors in the darkness, the Saskatchewans landed under cover of nautical twilight at 0455 hours, only five minutes late. Lieutenant Buchanan wrote:

> 'As our small boats crept into the shore we could see lights shining in some windows and smoke curling from a few chimneys. We thought how peaceful it was and how soon we would disturb this quiet sea-side town by rifle and gunfire.'

Unlike the Royals' delayed landing, the Saskatchewans' approach had been silent, and the landing, in a single wave, was undetected. The South Saskatchewans had achieved vital moments of surprise

Green Beach looking east. The River Scie discharges into the sea through the shingle bank.

A and D proposed

A and D actual

that were denied to the Royals on Blue Beach. Lieutenant Buchanan continued:

> 'Our steel-shod boots pounded on the heavy shingle beach. It sounded like thunder after the slapping of small waves against the side of our landing craft and the muffled throb of marine engines.'

By the time the first enemy machine guns opened fire, the assault companies had cut the barbed wire and, using scaling ladders, most of the Canadians were safely over the sea wall, ignoring the black boards fixed to the barbed wire marked in white paint with the word 'Minen.' Major McRae recalled that 'very few casualties occurred during the beach landing.' *Invicta's* Flotilla Officer, Lieutenant Murray, later reported,

> '. . . unopposed, except that LCA 315 which touched down two minutes later on the extreme right flank was fired upon by a light machine-gun post. Military personnel in this craft suffered several casualties as they disembarked.'

According to the official historian, some 'personal accounts suggested that the enemy had purposely held his fire until after the landing.' However, if this had been the German platoon commander's intention, then he was denying himself an opportunity to destroy the Saskatchewans on the beach: a natural killing area. The Battalion's adjutant, Lieutenant Buchanan, recalled that:

> 'It was a peaceful scene, but almost immediately my comfortable illusion was shattered when guns began to fire from emplacements in the cliffs. Tracer cracked over our heads and I heard one soldier shout cheerfully "Gee, this is better than the fourth of July!"'

With the Canadians off the beach, the Germans concentrated their fire on the withdrawing landing craft. However, as the Canadians moved inland, the battalion discovered that they had, in the darkness, landed much further to the right and on a much narrower frontage than had been planned. Of greatest significance, both A and D Companies were west of the River Scie rather than to the east. To reach their objectives they would have to either cross the inundated area via the bridge and causeway inland from the sea wall, or return to the fire-swept beach. This was a critical error, and in effect, it

**The German MP40 or *Schmeisser***

negated the tactical surprise that the SSRs had gained.

In among the houses of Pourville, their Special Platoon caught the German off-duty shift. The radar expert, Flight Sergeant Jack Nissental, described the scene:

*'A door banged open and half a dozen Germans ran out. One was pulling on his jacket, holding his* Schmeisser *machine gun in his other hand. Another tugged up his trousers as he ran. Smokey fired a long burst from his Sten and the Germans went down like rubber toys, waving arms and legs. Bullets ricocheted off the wall behind them.'*

Also surprised were some off-duty German officers and a number of local girls who had stayed over after an officers' mess party the evening before. Enjoying female company, the officers had ignored the commotion and firing as a 'routine clash that was nothing to do with them,' but they were disabused of this notion by Lieutenant McIlveen's platoon of C Company, whose task it was to clear the building. Locked doors burst open under the blows of rifle butts and steel-shod boots. Few of the half-dressed or naked officers and their orderlies ever reached their feet. The French girls screamed as the Canadians shot or bayoneted their erstwhile escorts. 'They rounded up five girls, some only wearing bras and panties, . . . sobbing in terror at the sight of violent and ugly death.' Shortly afterwards, a grinning corporal shepherded the partly-clad girls down to Battalion Headquarters. It is not clear whether these were the same girls who later worked alongside Canadian medics near the sea front, treating wounded soldiers.

Lieutenant Colonel Cecil Merritt VC

Meanwhile, Lieutenant Colonel

The bridge over the Scie and the view looking inland towards the Four Winds feature.

Merritt and his small Tactical Headquarters, who had landed alongside the assault companies, was making his way to the village garage, which was to be the battalion's first HQ. As they moved through the streets, cannon-firing Spitfires raked the enemy positions on the headlands. Flakes of brick, concrete and ricocheting lead zipped around the Canadians' ears as the Germans returned the fire. Corporal Red Sudds of the Special Platoon, who had earlier complained about his newly-issued Sten gun, was hit in the streets of Pourville. Jack Nissenthal recalled:

> 'He suddenly pitched forward as though he had seen something immensely valuable on the ground and must at all costs pick it up. I shouted at him but he did not answer. I shook him but he just rolled slackly on his side. He had grown a small hole like a birthmark over his right eye; it was rimmed with pink skin but the rest of his face looked sallow, the colour of wax. A little blood seeped out of the hole. He was dead.'

A French resident of Pourville braved the fire and told a Canadian infantryman sheltering by his front wall that 'the Germans had been waiting for you.' This statement conflicts with the belief that surprise was achieved at Green Beach. It may be that the elderly Frenchman was merely commenting on the overall state of alert that he had noted over the previous days.

## The Bridge

Once in the village, A and D Companies could not return to the beach, but had to cross the river in the centre of the town. Lance Corporal McKenzie wrote:

> 'We got over the wall and well into the town before we were fired on, which was at the concrete bridge over the river. The bridge was

*covered with fire from the hill to the left and made it very hard for us to get across. Some of our boys got over the bridge, some swam the river. I for one had a tough time swimming the river as my equipment dragged me down. As we crossed the river I heard mortar fire for the first time.'*

Others chose to rush the Bridge. Private Krohn recalled:

*'The main street was easy to be seen, so we dashed for it and turned left to cross the bridge. L/Cpl Chilton, Evenden, Carswell, Pickford and I were fired upon when we reached halfway across. Chilton, Evenden and Pickford made a mad dash for the other side; Carswell was wounded, together with two other boys beside me. It was too late for us to be able to make the dash. One more boy fell right beside me, so I flattened out, rolled myself over the side, into the Canal* [embanked river course] *at the same time dragging one of the boys with me. The bridge was under heavy fire by this time. The rest of the company had to wade the Canal.'*

At this point, the Saskatchewan's Commanding Officer intervened 'in the difficult situation to the east of the village.' Lieutenant Dickin, acting Intelligence officer, was at Battalion HQ, when it became clear that A and D Companies were 'having a stiff time.' Lieutenant Colonel Merritt, sensing a problem, moved to the key point of the battle. Approaching the bridge, he found Lieutenant Nesbitt, commanding 17 Platoon of D Company, who with some of his men was held up at the bridge by a machine gun firing on a fixed line. Lieutenant Nesbitt described how Colonel Merritt came up 'and decided we should dash over the bridge. He led the way and we crossed OK and I do not think we had any casualties.' Through the force of his own example, as described by Captain Carswell:

*'Lieutenant Colonel Merritt led several parties across the bridge in Pourville which was swept by machine-gun, mortar and field gun fire continually. He was constantly exposing himself. On many occasions he crossed over the bridge, urging his men forward and calling, "See, there is no danger here". The men followed him splendidly but were shot down time after time.'*

Lieutenant Edmondson tells of what he himself saw:

*'More than half of our Company were across the bridge when I arrived. The Colonel, when he saw we were being held up, crossed the bridge several times, urging the men forward, and the men followed. The dead were piled two deep for about 50 feet along the bridge.'*

The Germans were dug in on the high ground overlooking Pourville and the Scie Valley.

Lieutenant Colonel Merritt was awarded the first Canadian Victoria Cross of the Second World War for gallantry, when he 'personally led the survivors of at least four parties in turn across the bridge.' The problem at the crossing point was further eased when a pillbox sited to fire directly on to the bridge was temporarily silenced by 'anti-tank fire' from a Boys rifle.

The attack on the Four Winds feature.

## Four Winds Farm

With D Company across the bridge, Colonel Merritt organized a further advance under fire, during which 'he carried the men forward' with his leadership, led an attack right up to a pillbox, and threw grenades inside. Sergeant McBride described the inspiring example set by his commanding officer:

> 'The first time I met the Colonel, we were over the bridge. There was heavy fire coming down on the road as I joined a group of men who were held up. I heard the Colonel speak and he said, "We must get ahead, lads, we need more men up front as quick as possible. Who's coming with me?" I replied, "We are all going with you." He said, "Good lads, let's go." We ran up the road with Colonel

Merritt leading: disregarding all danger, he led us straight up the road, and after about 40 yards he stopped. Soon the Colonel said, "Are you ready again?" We answered, "O.K. Sir," and away we went again right up to the roadblock. There we left Colonel Merritt and went to rejoin A Company.'

In spite of the Commanding Officer's gallantry, D Company, who were pushing on towards their hill-top objective, Four Winds Farm, were 'frustrated by the enemy's mortar and machine gun fire.' Lance Sergeant Coldwell described a right-flanking attack led by Major McTavish in which Private Fenner:

'...crawled up the hill and walked straight into the enemy positions, firing a Bren gun from his hip and reached the top of the hill killing a considerable amount of Germans... At this point Private Fenner was wounded very badly, being shot in both legs... We dragged him down the hill on his back where we dressed his wounds.'

D Company only secured a foothold on Four Winds feature, and was unable to hold their gains in the face of concentrated fire from across the valley and from further in land. A major factor in this set back was the arrival of a cyclist platoon from the 571 *Infanteries* reserve, who had arrived well ahead of their comrades who were marching to the battle. Their arrival firmly tipped the balance of forces against the Canadians. Having withdrawn back to the foot of the hill, D Company were redeployed to support A Company, who were similarly struggling to take the radar station.

### The Radar Station

Having been delayed for about twenty minutes by the marshy flooded area that the Germans had created behind the sea wall, A Company's progress up on to the high ground to the east was

**The view inland from the cliffs to the east of Green Beach.**

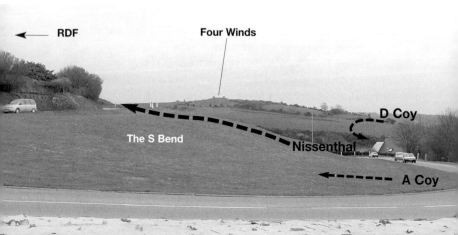

**A trench line still visible in the area of the Radar Station.**

checked by a road block covered by enemy fire. Looking up the slope towards the radar site, Major Murray Osten's soldiers could see the tall radar antenna of Freyer 28 still rotating, as it had been before dawn when it had detected the approaching Allied shipping. However, with some two hundred yards of open terrain to cross and a number of active German positions covering the ground, A Company were also pinned down and killed. They needed mortar-fire support, but none was available, and the observation officers' request for naval gunfire support did not get through. However, MGB 317 and two landing-craft support were engaging targets that they could identify as enemy. Overhead, RAF and *Luftwaffe* fighters were fighting their own battle, and empty cases and spent bullets rained down on the infantrymen below.

Flight Sergeant Nissenthal was sheltering in a ditch with his escort; he described the situation that faced A Company:

*'I raised my head cautiously and scanned the hill to see how other SSRs were faring. Near the concrete roadblock, the road was dotted with bodies, some wearing khaki and some in field grey. None was moving. Around them lay the detritus of dead soldiers; a litter of rifles, steel helmets, smoke canisters; an abandoned two-inch mortar, a smashed radio set. I could hear shouts of orders and counter-orders, the rattle of machine guns, the crack of rifles and the hollow thump of mortars. Whether they were Canadian or German, it was impossible to know.'*

The concrete radar position was surrounded by a high blast-wall that was faced by an earth-and-sandbag bank. Around the radar casemate were trenches and machine-gun positions, and rolls of concertina wire piled twelve feet high surrounded the whole site.

141

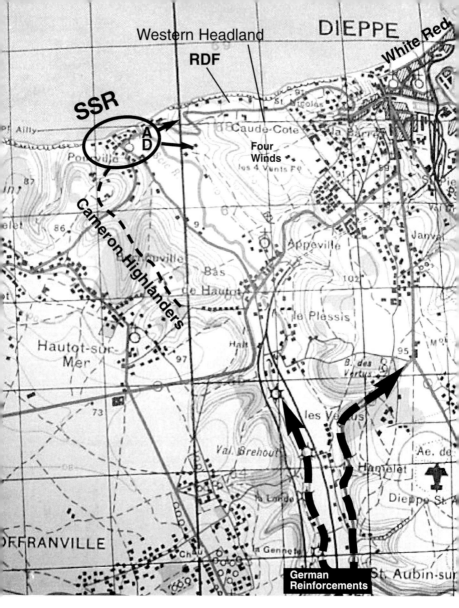

**The area inland from Green Beach.**

Assembling such firepower as they had, A Company, reinforced by 10 and 12 Platoons from B Company, gave covering fire to the Special Platoon, who attempted to crawl forward across the broken ground towards the radar site. However, the Germans, too numerous to be suppressed by the Canadians' fire, spotted them, and Jack Nissenthal and his escort were driven back in the face of growing German firepower. Some time later, after further vain attempts to get naval or artillery support, Sergeant Nissenthal decided to attempt to reach the radar on his own, covered by the fire of all the available Canadians.

Under the noses of the German defenders, who could be seen manning the trenches, Nissenthal stealthily made his way around to an unguarded flank and into the radar site. With the German defender's attention focused on keeping A Company away from the site, Nissenthal was able to cut the cables coming out of the Freyer casemate. By doing this, he provided valuable information.

During the previous autumn, British radio-interception stations on the south coast, monitoring German radio communications, regularly picked up coded messages from Freya operators. British cryptographers broke these codes, and revealed that the messages were to command posts, giving details of approaching aircraft. From this data, British radar technicians were able to calculate the capabilities of the chain of German RDF stations. However, when the Germans connected the radar sites by telephone, this useful source of intelligence stopped. By cutting these telephone lines, Jack had forced the radar operators of Freyer Number 28, which was tracking the largest air engagement of the war over France to date, to resort to easily-intercepted radio to pass on details of incoming Allied air attacks.

Radio-intercept stations along the South Coast recorded, decoded and analysed the German radio messages. From this text and from known movements of Allied Air Forces, the scientists were able to gage the extent of the developments to the Freyer system during the nine months since the regular coded messages had ceased. This information, though not as useful as a full internal examination of the system or the seizure of parts, was a significant factor in the technical war that was being fought by scientists.

### The German Reaction

As with D Company, A Company had been unable to take its objectives on the Western Headland. 8 *Kompanie* was proving to be a determined enemy. It is interesting to speculate what might have resulted if tanks of the Calgary Regiment had been landed at Pourville, as had been envisaged in the early versions of the Rutter plan. Lacking sufficient combat power, the SSR's attack on the high ground was broken off, and the companies concentrated on holding the ground already gained. This was easier said than done, as the

well-exercised German defensive plan was producing a much swifter reaction than had been expected.

The reserves of 571 *Infanterie* Regiment were awoken and placed on notice to move at 0530 hours. The leading elements of 1st Battalion relied on bicycles for mobility. In theory, this means of transport had worked well on exercise, but when, after an hour's frenetic preparations, they set out with a full combat load of ammunition, the reality was rather different. The leading *Kompanie* on its eight mile march to Pourville was plagued with punctures, as under pressure of the heavily-laden infantrymen, the spokes became unseated. The march took a full three hours.

Meanwhile, back in Pourville, Colonel Merritt was forced to move his Tactical Headquarters, as it was being unerringly engaged by mortar fire. One theme consistently mentioned in Canadian accounts of Green Beach is a theory that the Germans had used radio direction-finding equipment to locate their HQ positions accurately and to use this as targeting information. This may be true, as the Germans used such equipment to detect French Resistance radio operators. However, from positions overlooking Pourville, they could also have located the Canadians with the naked eye.

Casualties from mortar fire included Regimental Sergeant Major Strumm, a Great War veteran, who suffered a serious wound to his leg. Though already wounded, he narrowly avoided death but his polished-steel field-shaving mirror in his breast pocket prevented his heart from being pierced by a razor-sharp shell splinter. The RSM was evacuated, saying as he went, 'They told me I was too old to get into action,

**FRANÇAIS!**

Ceci est un coup de main et non pas l'invasion.

Nous vous prions instamment de n'y prendre part en aucune façon et de ne faire quoi que ce soit qui puisse entraîner des représailles de la part de l'ennemi.

Nous faisons appel à votre sang-froid et à votre bon sens.

Lorsque l'heure sonnera, nous vous avertirons. C'est alors que nous agirons côte-à-côte pour notre victoire commune et pour votre liberté!

A copy of the leaflet dropped by Allied aircraft as the raid began warning the French that this was only a raid.

The panoramic view from just below the RDF site, across the Scie Valley to the high ground where the Queen's Own Cameron Highlanders advanced inland.

but I fooled em.'

Despite leaflets warning the people of Pourville that this was not the invasion and that they should not compromise themselves, a number of French men and women actively supported the Canadians. Many accounts commented on the number of old gentlemen, no doubt veterans of the Great War, who stood calmly watching the exchange of small-arms fire, ignoring the detonation of shells. Most fondly remembered of all were the young French women who brought succour to the growing number of wounded at the Regimental Aid Post. Although they knew the risks of being seen cooperating with the Canadians, they insisted on helping, and help was sorely needed. They pressed water and wine to the lips of the wounded and passed around fruit to the men bringing in their wounded comrades. In general, however, it is worth noting that the French heeded the Allies' warnings and remained at least neutral. The Germans acknowledged this by releasing French POWs from Dieppe captured in 1940 to their families.

## Queen's Own Cameron Highlanders

The Camerons, travelling in twenty-five LCP(L)s from Newhaven, landed half an hour late at 0550 hours, as a result of a navigational error. With the enemy now fully alert, still manning untaken positions that covered the beach, Lieutenant Colonel Gostling and his men received the full effect of the enemy's fire. With Piper Alex Graham playing 'The Hundred Pipers' standing on the bow of a landing craft, shells started bursting around the Camerons during their final run-in to the beach. The landings were made astride the mouth of the River Scie, which had considerable influence on subsequent events. According to Colonel Stacey:

'LCP(L) 129, in Mr. O'Rourke's phrase, "hit the objective in a rather awkward position," at the east end of

145

Green Beach, east of the outlet of the River Scie, and not far from a German pill-box which was still in action, the one beach position which the S Sask R had not succeeded in clearing. Lieutenant Colonel Gostling went ashore and began to direct the battalion's advance through the wire obstacles.'

The Commanding Officer was 'directing wire cutting' when he was shot down and killed by a burst of fire from a *Spandau* in a pillbox built into the headland. Major Law, the battalion's Second-in-Command, stated that, 'the parts of the unit that landed west of the river got across the sea wall with little difficulty and few casualties, which is in contrast to those who landed to the east [D and parts of B and C Companies], which the Saskatchewans had not been able to clear, and were held up for a time.'

Once the Camerons were in the cover of Pourville, Major Law, as described in their war diary, reviewed the situation:

'It became evident, from the amount of mortar and shellfire coming on Pourville, that the enemy were aware that there were now two battalions in the town. A hasty appreciation of the situation and discussion with the SSR's HQ revealed that the SSRs were held up by two pillboxes, which controlled the crossing of the River Scie. Parts of D Coy had worked their way around the right flank of the bridge and were in a good fire position. In view of this, it was decided to leave D Coy to support the SSRs and adopt our alternative route to the aerodrome, our objective i.e. via the west side of the River Scie.'

The Camerons, with A Company in the lead, set off to their objective of the St Aubin airfield and the reported divisional headquarters location. Their first task was to seize a bridge at Bas-du-Hautot and reach their rendezvous with the tanks of the Calgary Regiment. However, 'while proceeding south along the axis of the road Pourville – Bas-du-Hautot, we came under heavy mortar and MG fire from the area of les 4 Vents Farm on the east side of the river.' Once in the cover of Bois d'Hautot, 'we were not bothered by any mortar or machine-gun fire from this point onwards.'

Once through the wood, the battalion deployed into an open formation and continued to move south across open ground.

According to the report in the war diary:

*'A considerable amount of* [enemy] *activity along the road was seen, generally moving north on the west side of the river and moving south on the east side of the river. The time was now approximately 0845 hours and up to this time no information from Brigade had been received. The tanks, which by now should have been patrolling near us could not be seen . . . Time was getting short . . . therefore it was decided to abandon our original objectives. Strong enemy forces were coming up along the road. These were engaged by Bn HQ and the support platoon. Heavy casualties were inflicted on the enemy and they eventually withdrew.'*

Three horse-drawn close-support infantry guns were seen attempting to cross a bridge, but the range was too great for effective rifle fire. As the Camerons had lost their mortar platoon during the landing, they had to rely on short bursts from Bren guns and 2-inch mortar 'to keep them down.' This artillery detachment seen moving towards Dieppe was, according to the German report, grouped with the reserve of 571 *Infanterie* Regiment consisting of 'a cyclist platoon and patrols from the 1st Battalion.' Meanwhile, A Company successfully located and destroyed an enemy mortar platoon, along with another horse-drawn mortar detachment that was moving forward to join the battle. But by around 0800 hours, the number of German reserves converging on Dieppe was growing significantly.

With their original plan abandoned, the Camerons were planning to attack the Four Winds Farm from the rear when a radio message from Headquarters 6 Brigade was finally received at about 0900 hours. 'Vanquish from Green Beach at 1030 hrs.' 'Vanquish' was the code word for withdrawal, and it was to be via Pourville, rather than the main Dieppe beach as planned. What was going on in Dieppe? They all wondered.

### The Withdrawal from Green Beach

The Cameron's war diary reports:

*'The withdrawal commenced under heavy fire at 0930 hrs. The Pioneer Platoon and Support Platoon acted as a vanguard; flank*

A photograph of the Coastal profile model as issued to the Saskatchewan

*protection was supplied by A Coy; C Coy fought the rear-guard action.*

*'Enemy snipers harassed us but the main body was ably protected by the rear guard, whose casualties were heavy. We were soon under the protection of Bernouville Woods and a rapid withdrawal to Pourville was affected. Enemy machine-gun and mortar fire covering the road immediately south of Pourville inflicted further casualties upon us.'*

As they approached the defended perimeter, the Camerons were met by a platoon-sized patrol of Saskatchewans, who had been sent out to help them break clean and carry out a passage of lines into the Pourville beachhead. Arriving in the village at 0956 hours, they were informed that the LCAs 'that were to take us off the beach would not be arriving until 1100 hrs' rather than 1030 hours as previously advised. With this delay and the growing pressure from the German force that had followed them back to the beachhead, Major Orme decided to deploy A and B Companies to help the Saskatchewans stop the enemy advance onto the high ground west of Pourville.

The net result of a delay in passing on information was that the Canadians abandoned the high ground to the west and withdrew prematurely because of time considerations based on faulty information. The Germans, despite belated attempts to check them, occupied positions overlooking Green Beach. This had a profound effect on the evacuation and caused the heavy casualties that the Saskatchewans and Camerons suffered during the withdrawal.

The Saskatchewan's withdrawal from below the RDF site and the slopes of the Four Winds Farm feature was potentially very difficult, and had to be carefully controlled if the men were not to break and run. War correspondent Wallace Reyburn was with Battalion Headquarters, and later wrote:

*'As we set off along the road to the promenade I heard Merritt's voice, "Don't run, men. Slope arms and march to the beach." I saw the man in front of me shoulder his rifle and start marching. I'd been dashing forward in a crouching position, hoping that I'd be less of a target for the snipers but automatically I raised myself erect and marched with the other men around me.'*

Following behind Colonel Merritt's men, the Germans occupied the Canadians' abandoned positions and then pressed on downhill, but were halted by the SSR's fire from the houses at the edge of Pourville. The two sides now engaged in a small-arms duel and, despite the Camerons' earlier success in knocking out mortar positions, the volume of medium mortar bombs targeted at the town increased sharply.

Colonel Stacey recorded that 'At 1040 hrs Brigadier Mann informed Uxbridge that LCAs were "going to GREEN [Beach] PETER [Sector] for Cecil [SSRs] and Goose [Camerons]". The first LCAs touched down on the beach at approximately1104 hours. Colonel Stacey continues:

> 'The evidence of every witness is that as soon as the troops began to cross the beach, which due to the state of the tide was now 200 yards wide, a very heavy cross-fire... came down upon it. It appears that this fire included that of mortars, machine guns and small arms, and there is some evidence that there was shellfire also. Lieutenant Commander Prior [RN] had made very efficient preparations for evacuation, having the barbed wire cleared away and the casualties placed under cover ready to be removed. Some of the enemy prisoners, who were comparatively numerous in this area, were used as stretcher-bearers and did good work as such.'

In spite of this, very few stretcher cases could be evacuated, and of the prisoners, only one was brought back to England. The Camerons reported that they suffered the majority of their casualties during the withdrawal phase. Bodies littered the beach as groups of men dashed across the fire-swept strand.

The waiting landing craft, shrouded in protective smoke, broke cover and headed in to the beach. Ross Munro, who had earlier witnessed the disaster at Blue Beach, was with an LCA flotilla that

Pourville and the high ground to the west of Green Beach that was abandoned too soon.

**Canadian evacuees, mainly wounded, are transferred from an LCA to one of the destroyers.**

was now dispatched to assist with the withdrawal from Green Beach.

> 'The landing craft now were moving in on Pourville, scores of them circling slowly off shore and then turning in to the beach, many of them grounding before they got there. The S.S.R. and Camerons came across the beach through the machine-gun fire and raced for the boats. They brought all the casualties they could. They even brought some prisoners.

> 'I was in an assault boat, which tried to go into Pourville; we got within three hundred yards of the beach when we were ordered along the coast to try to make the main beach and take off troops there. But I did get a glimpse of the Pourville evacuation.'

On the beach, the Cameron's Adjutant was attempting to control the re-embarkation of his battalion:

> 'From this moment on, the enemy machine guns and mortars ranged on the beach and brought down a murderous fire. One LCA, which was loaded, grounded on the beach, and the troops had to get out and push. It was shelled and one shell penetrated near the bow, making it unserviceable. The enemy machine guns took advantage

and mowed down everybody in the vicinity. Another LCA was so badly damaged and was so overloaded that it capsized. This one unfortunately contained a number of casualties. Two LCAs managed to clear the beach successfully.

'A few minutes later, one LCT and three more LCAs arrived. More troops were sent down, and again the enemy machine guns opened up, causing terrific casualties.'

The view from seawards was no better. Ross Munro wrote:

'It wasn't any nice ordered sight. The boats were having trouble. Many of them were under direct machine-gun fire. Some were sinking, with troops leaping back into the water. Batches of Canadians were on the fringe of the town among some trees on the inside of the sea wall. Small groups of them hesitated there for a while; then they would leap over the sea wall to the beach and scatter for the run over the pebbles to the water and the boats. There was the hammering sound of German machine-guns, the occasional sharp whang of the mortars and the knock knock of the Brens. Smoke drifted over the beach in a long wispy trail as our craft turned for the main beach.'

With the re-embarkation clearly not going well, the Hunt Class destroyers HMS *Albrington* and HMS *Brockelsby*, along with gunboats, came as close into the beach as they dared and gave covering fire to the Canadians. Under this cover, the Camerons and SSRs swam out to the LCAs and MGBs, whose crews were also suffering heavily from enemy fire. 'Again the enemy machine guns fired on us and several were hit while swimming.' Lieutenant Commander Hanson of HMS *Albrington* reported:

'During the final withdrawal from Green Beach, men were seen lying under the sea wall and dashing down under fire to the sea. Permission to bombard flanks was obtained from HMS Calpe and the position of some enemy forces in houses to right of beach was established from soldiers who had been brought off. Smoke shell was also fired onto the high ground to right of beach. Afterwards, this ship picked up stragglers and survivors until the retirement was ordered. During the withdrawal [visual signalling] communication was difficult due to great quantities of smoke. Coastal and landing craft were making for the nearest destroyer asking for instructions, which were difficult to give.'

HMS *Albrighton* recovered a total of 182 soldiers and landing craft crews, 'as well as eight who died' of their wounds.

## The Last Stand of the Saskatchewans

Lieutenant Colonel Merrit had already repeatedly heroically led groups of his men across the bridge, but throughout the withdrawal to Green Beach, his per-sonal leadership, courage and example of selfless commitment was to inspire his men to the heights of sacrifice. He and other leaders of all ranks, includ-ing Lieutenant Commander Prior of the Royal Navy, elected to remain behind to mount a rear-guard action, even though they could have saved themselves from death, wounds or capture. The Saskatchewan's Adjutant, Lieutenant Buchanan, recalled that his Commanding Officer was one of the few men in the battalion who was a strong swimmer and could easily have saved himself.

> 'Major McRae said to him, "Come on, get the hell out of here." But Merritt, he was a bulldog. These were his men. He was only a young fellow and this was such a disaster, he must have been torn to pieces inside. He started off, but then he said, "Oh God; my job is back there" and he swam back to the beach. So he stayed there. . .'

If his earlier action at the bridge had not been enough to ensure he would be awarded a VC, Colonel Merritt, under heavy fire, ran across the beach to drag wounded men from the sea back into the cover of the seawall. Captain Runcie said of this and other acts of heroism, 'It wasn't human, what he did'. During this part of the battle, the Colonel, seemingly immune from enemy fire, was finally hit but he carried on despite his wound.

With the last few craft coming in, and a rapidly diminishing number of unwounded Canadians waiting on the beach, Colonel Merritt, Major Claude Orme and a group of soldiers fought on in the casino, covering what was to be the final withdrawal, but hoping that more LCAs and support would come to their rescue. There was to be no further evacuation, and during the course of the afternoon, as ammunition ran out, the Germans cautiously advanced towards the casino on the sea front that had been Colonel

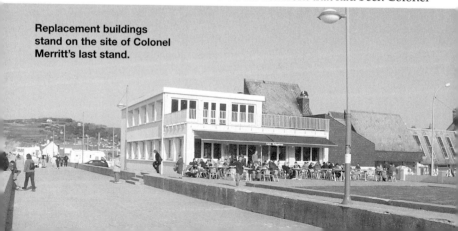

**Replacement buildings stand on the site of Colonel Merritt's last stand.**

Canadian wounded being helped to safety.

Safe aboard a ship but harrowed looks mark the faces of the men who were lucky enought to escape from the beaches.

Merritt's last defence. All around, there were dead and wounded Canadians.

The Combined Operations report stated that 'in spite of the extremely difficult conditions, a very considerable number of men were successfully withdrawn'. But the casualties on Green Beach and Pourville were high. Of the 523 SSR who set off to Dieppe, 84 were killed or died of wounds; 89 became prisoners of war; and of the 353 who returned to England, 167 were wounded. The Camerons, who embarked a total of 503 men at Newhaven, recovered only 268 men back to England, including 103 wounded. Sixty Camerons were killed and a further sixteen died in British or German hospitals, while 167 became PoWs. The troops landing at Green Beach had lost more than sixty-five per cent of their strength.

Some time later, in a prisoner-of-war camp in Germany, Lieutenant Colonel Merritt received news from the German Camp Commandant that he had been awarded the Victoria Cross, Canada's highest award for bravery. A fellow South Saskatchewan prisoner had just received a swatch of maroon material cut from the cloth used to cover his favourite couch back in Canada. With a medal ribbon made up with this swatch, the prisoners held what must be the most unusual and unofficial investiture ever.

**One of the few prisoners of war taken back to England in the hands of a military policeman.**

# CHAPTER EIGHT

# DIEPPE – RED AND WHITE BEACHES

The German response to the preliminary landings at 0445 hours, to east and west of Dieppe, was prompt, but there was the usual uncertainty, because some initial situation reports based on assumptions or scant information proved to be incorrect. Reports climbed the German chain of command, and a message from HQ *LXXXI Korps* to Fifteenth Army, timed 0605 hours, read 'Bombs dropping on Dieppe, and enemy landing attempts at Berneval, Dieppe, Pourville and Quiberville.' At 0630 hours, *General-Feldmarschall* von Rundstedt was at his desk in GHQ West, receiving a similar message.

*Feldmarschall* **von Rundstedt.**

Initially, von Rundstedt was by no means clear how the action around Dieppe fitted into the overall picture. It was however, obvious to him from the outset that if this was just a raid, it was certainly the largest raid of the war so far, with coordinated landings on a frontage of about fifteen miles. Alternatively, these landings could be the first move in the major invasion that the *Abwehr* had so confidently predicted. Von Rundstedt waited for further detailed 'Sitreps' to arrive, but none came. At 0700 hours, without further confirmation of Allied intentions, he ordered Fifteenth Army to bring 10th Panzer Division and the SS Adolf Hitler Division to Alarm Scale Z. He also requested the *Luftwaffe* to be prepared to intercept the Allied air forces that were bound to be active over northern France. Finally, though it was promptly rejected, he requested the *Kriegsmarine* to mount U-boat attacks on the Allied amphibious force.

At 0732 hours, the Sitreps eventually started to arrive. Chief of Staff, HQ *LXXXI Korps* reported that 'the landing attempt at Pourville had been repelled, but bombing continued on Dieppe.' The situation at Quiberville was, however, 'still unclear,' and at

0740 hours, the *Kriegesmarine* reported that telephone lines to the port commandant at Dieppe were cut. This forced the Naval Signal Station at Dieppe to transmit a message by radio: 'English continue to land at Dieppe. Destroyers laying smoke on coast. Up to now twelve tanks have landed. One is on fire'. *Oberst* Bartlet, commanding 571 *Infanterie* Regiment, realising that the attack was concentrated around Dieppe, had already ordered I Battalion his regimental reserve to advance on Pourville from the west and south-west at 0710 hours.

General Kuntzen, commander *LXXXI Korps*, at his headquarters at Canteleu near Rouen, was convinced from an early stage that the enemy attack was purely a raid, and correctly assessed the enemy operation as lacking sufficient combat power to be a credible spearhead of a full invasion. He therefore ordered his reserve of four lorried infantry battalions to converge on Dieppe.

Shortly afterwards at 0730 hours, the 10th Panzer Division joined *Korps* and 302nd Division's reserves in marching towards Dieppe. The first reinforcements, an infantry *Kampfgruppe* based ten miles from the port, arrive in the Dieppe area in time to be in action at 0800 hours. It is this *Kampfgruppe* that the Camerons had clashed with near Petit Appeville. However, moving on pre-recced routes it was appreciated that it would take most of the reserves at least four hours to fully concentrate in the Dieppe area, and longer for them to recce enemy positions, routes and forming-up places, prior to coming into action.

**German Panzers on the march in France. 10th Panzer Division did not arrive until after the Canadian withdrawal.**

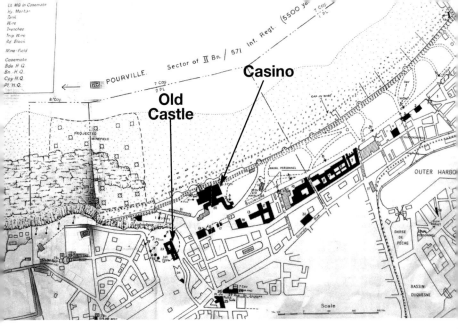

Old
Castle

Casino

← POURVILLE

**(Above) A map of the defences compiled after the raid.**

**(Right) One of the postcards used to brief the Canadian troops. The view is looking east from the Western Headland along the main beach to the harbour entrance.**

## The Defenders of Dieppe

II Battalion 571 *Infanterie* Regiment held the town of Dieppe, as far east as the entrance to the port and the headland, and as far west as Pourville; in all, a frontage of 5,500 yards. To the east of the harbour, III Battalion held the Eastern Headland, and were strung out along the coastline as far east as the small port, le Treport. A part of I Battalion was deployed on the coast to the west of the port, with, as already noted, an infantry company as reserve further inland.

The mile-long Esplanade was mainly held by the 150 men of 7 *Kompanie*, of whom many were *Volksdeutsch* from captured territories in the east, or simply foreigners who, finding themselves citizens of Greater Germany, had been conscripted into the *Wehrmacht*. Along with a number of *Kriegsmarine* anti-tank gunners, they occupied positions in pillboxes along the seawall, and also occupied strong points such as the Casino and the Old Castle (at the western end of what was to be White Beach). Their task was to fire onto the beach and to cover the sea wall and the wire obstacles along its top. The sea wall at this time varied in height from just a few feet to its full ten feet, according to how the sea had banked the shingle and how effectively the Germans had bulldozed it back again. The double barbed-wire fence, made up of multiple rolls of dannert wire, was some seven feet thick, with a fifteen-foot gap between the two entanglements. This combination of sea wall and the wire fences was a significant obstacle that would have to be breached before any force of infantry or tanks could get off the beach. Beyond the beach defences lay the open grass lawn of the Esplanade; 7 *Kompanie's* killing area. Here, any force attempting to cross the sixty yards of open ground to attack them and press on into the town would be caught in a crossfire from strong points, supplemented by riflemen and *Spandau* gunners positioned in the large houses and hotels that backed the Esplanade. The defensive positions in the already substantial buildings had, according to the

(Left) The Old Castle still stands overlooking the medieval gate and the site of the Casino.

(Below) The view from across the Esplanade Boulevard Marechal Foch to the lawns and Boulevard de Verdun and the substantial buildings beyond.

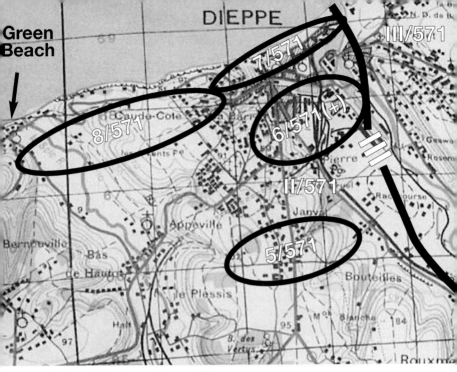

**II/571 Infantry's Deployment Around Dieppe.**

post-operational intelligence analysis, 'been fortified by masonry and/or concrete blocks.'

In defences around the port area were the naval ratings of 3rd *Kompanie* of the Experimental Battalion (Naval). The infantry of 8 *Kompanie* held positions on the dominating Western Headland, including Four Winds Farm, while 6 *Kompanie* and other *Kriegsmarine* troops held the town and port facilities. Finally, 5 *Kompanie* was guarding the inland approaches to the town, with the role of immediate reserve in the case of a frontal attack.

To the infantry's small-arms fire must be added that of the artillery positions on the cliffs to east and west, along with their mortar detachments located further inland. The Germans had even concreted into position a captured French R17-18 tank, with a 37mm gun, on the harbour wall at the eastern end of Red Beach. This gun and coaxial machine gun could fire down the entire length of the beach, and caused significant problems to the Canadians.

In summary, Dieppe was a very strong defensive position, which Combined Operations had elected to assault in a frontal attack. However, there were not many Germans in the town, as some reports and commentators have indicated. German records,

159

confirmed by interrogation of the handful of German prisoners taken back to England, are explicit: there was a single infantry battalion in the town. What did surprise the Allies was the speed with which Germans from the surrounding area were able to start concentrating on Dieppe.

### The Ground

The Jubilee plans were based on an analysis of the beach and the immediate area inland, which was detailed in the COHQ report:

*'The beach stretches from the breakwater for 1,700 yards. The high-water line is backed by a seawall about ten feet high, from which numerous groynes run out into the sea. The beach itself is composed of shingle four inches in diameter, or less, sloping down to sand at the low-water line. For the first 130 yards, the gradient of the beach is 1 in 40, then it rises steeply (1 in 10) to the seawall. The average width of the beach is 130 yards, but at its western end, it is somewhat more than 300 yards. The seawall, built of masonry and concrete, is 1,500 yards long with a vertical face... Immediately behind this sea wall and running for its whole length, is the* Boulevard Marechal Foch *[and]... beyond it are lawns and flowerbeds 165 feet wide, interspersed by paths. On the landward side of these lawns runs the* Boulevard de Verdun, *a road wide enough for two or three lines of traffic. The shingle has, in places, been washed up against the seawall almost level with its top. It was thought that nowhere was the top of the sea wall more than two feet above the beach shingle except*

**The western end of the beach was dominated by the large Casino building and the whole area, particularly to the west was overlooked by cliff's and the Old Castle.**

**Le Pollet or Eastern Headland**

Red Beach

**Dieppe's port area showing Red Beach, and the various basins beyond.**

*opposite the Casino and south-west towards the end of the promenade, where the height was about four feet. At five places along the seawall there were steps leading to the beach.'*

The western end of the beach was dominated by the large Casino building, and the whole area, particularly to the west, was overlooked by cliffs and the Old Castle.

### The Assault Plan

The initial assault was to be by two battalions of 4 Canadian Infantry Brigade, supported by the Calgary Regiment's Churchill tanks. The Essex Scottish were to land on the left (Red Beach) and the Royal Hamilton Light Infantry (RHLI) were to land on White Beach to the right. The landing was timed for 0520 hours, with the first flight of the Calgary Regiment's tanks touching down amongst the assault infantry. Their orders stressed 'It is vital to the success of the operation as a whole that White and Red Beaches be in our hands with the minimum delay.' The first wave of assault infantry were to establish a bridgehead, while supporting troops including military police would provide off-loading parties for the Royal Canadian Engineers' assault detachments. The COHQ report recorded:

161

> 'The latter would clear the necessary beach roadways and remove obstacles to enable the tanks to enter the town. The tanks, the order stated, would support the assault, and were to proceed to their objectives whether the beaches were cleared or not.'

However, there was an agreement that some of the tanks of the Calgary Regiment would assist the Beach Assault Engineers in their additional task of clearing pillboxes on the seawall.

The Essex Scottish, commanded by Lieutenant Colonel Jasperson, code named 'Fred,' having crossed Red Beach and the Esplanade, were to dispatch a company to the Bassin du Canada. They were to seize the bridges to the north and south of the basin, clear the east bank of the harbour, capture three light anti-aircraft guns on the Le Pollet (eastern) cliffs and then link up with the Royal Regiment of Canada, who were landing at Blue Beach. Another company was to seize the German armed trawlers at the quayside, with the assistance of the tanks, HMS *Locust* and a flotilla of French *Chasseur* craft, who would enter the harbour. This company would then help to clear and hold the east bank of the harbour. The third company was to remain on the west side of the harbour and capture anti-aircraft and artillery positions in that area. Subsequently, this company would secure the Hippodrome on the southern sector of the perimeter, and then select and mark an emergency airfield for the Air Force. Meanwhile, engineer demolition parties would be at work in the docks.

The Royal Hamilton Light Infantry, commanded by Lieutenant Colonel Labatt, code named 'Bob,' was according to Colonel Stacey to have:

> '...one company, moving west along the cliff-top from the Casino, to capture two Light AA guns near the edge of the cliff... and make contact with the South Saskatchewan Regiment [SSR] from Pourville. One troop of tanks was to cooperate. Subsequently this company would assist in the capture of the position at Les 4 Vents [Four Winds Farm].'

Another company, operating southward, was to capture the important battery position at a mile and a half inland and the three light anti-aircraft guns nearby. This company would also join the attack on Four Winds Farm. It will be recalled that in the event, without the support of the RHLI, the South Saskatchewan failed in their solitary attack from the west. The RHLI's third company was to operate southwards along Rue Gambetta as far as the southern edge of the town. Having reached these positions, the RHLI would secure the south-western perimeter of Dieppe, while the remainder of the battalion would be in reserve near battalion headquarters at the St Remy church.

The Calgary Regiment, commanded by Lieutenant Colonel Andrews, code named 'Johnny,' were to land in four flights. Flight One, consisting of nine tanks, would land at 0520 hours as follows: headquarters of C Squadron and 13 Troop were to land simultaneously with the Essex Scottish on Red Beach, while 8 Troop of B Squadron would land on White Beach, in support of the RHLI. Further tanks landing at 0535 hours were to support the Hamilton's part in the attack on Four Winds Farm, while the final flight of tanks would land at 0705 hours as a reserve and would 'probably exploit to Arques.'

The Canadian's floating reserve were les Fusiliers Mont-Royal, who, ready in their landing craft, were prepared to be deployed from 0650 hours. The Commanding Officer, Lieutenant Colonel Menard, was to report to HMS *Calpe* for orders, but 'If the operation went according to plan,' he had been warned, 'his task was to provide a rearguard on the western side of the harbour to cover the re-embarkation.'

The Royal Marine Commando (later re-designated 40 Commando) and naval personnel were to mount a cutting-out operation to take and tow away enemy shipping and invasion barges found in the port. This part of the operation depended on their being able to open the lock gates and operate the swing bridges.

## The Assault

The vessels carrying the assaulting force, HMS *Glengyle*, *Prince Leopold* and *Prince Charles*, reached their landing-craft-lowering positions on time, without contact with enemy shipping. The landing craft were lowered from the mother-ships' davits, and formed up correctly with none of the navigational difficulties that beset some of the other groups. As a result, the landing craft's run-in to the beach was uneventful.

Meanwhile, in contrast to the 'silent' or unsupported flanking attacks mounted by the commandos and the Canadians on the two inner flanking beaches, four of the Hunt Class destroyers began a covering bombardment with their guns. HMS *Garth* opened fire on the Esplanade at 0512 hours and shifted her aim to the eastern side of the harbour at 0519 hours, while HMS *Bleasdale* fired on the Casino and adjacent buildings between 0513 and 0520 hours. HMS *Berkeley* and *Albrighton* fired on the fortified buildings across the Esplanade from 0510 hours.

While the Navy was bombarding Dieppe, the Royal Air Force was also in action. COHQ reported that:

'*The smokescreen over the east headland was duly laid. The*

**(Below) A sketch of the Dieppe coastline issued to the Naval Force to help with navigation.**

Semaphore | Signal Station | Power Station | Tobacco Factory | Cathedral | St Remy Church Casino | Old Castle
Notre Dame de bon Secours | **Eastern Headland** | | Hotel Metropole Hotel Royal | | **Western Headland** |

*Air Force Commander states, "This was most effective, lasting from 0510 to 0600 hours." The attack by cannon fighters was also put in on schedule and was "successful in neutralizing enemy fire along the front from 0515 to 0525".'*

**Smoke from the bombardment of Dieppe, seen from a landing craft.**

However, many Canadians would later question how 'successful' and 'effective' this light bombardment was. Private Carley of the Essex Scottish, aboard an LCA heading for Red beach, recorded that

> *'We moved in until we were a half a mile from the shore directly in front of the town. We stopped as the RAF was just starting to bomb the town. We waited in our LCA till 14 minutes past five, as that was when the RAF stopped bombing. Then we moved into the beach.'*

With the air bombardment over, the landing craft continued their approach to the beach under cover of the smoke bombs dropped on the eastern headland. As they closed on the beach, the landing-crafts' smoke mortars fired on to the Esplanade. However, according to Lieutenant Commander McMullen, who navigated the force into Red and White beaches, 'fire appeared to be coming at us from every direction, but the boats touched down on the

German MG 34 positioned in a concrete casemate.

beach at 0523'. The force landed accurately, but the gap between the Essex Scottish at the eastern end of the beach and the RHLI in front of the Casino was greater than intended. Overhead, five close-support fighter squadrons had finished attacking the Dieppe seafront, but 'the fact that the infantry were a few minutes late prevented their taking full advantage of this attack.' This lack of effective coordination would explain many of the accusations from the survivors of the initial assault on the main Beaches, of a lack of support.

Even as the LCAs approached the beach, they were under increasingly heavy fire. Private Carley recalled that at 'about two hundred yards away from the beach, a terrible amount of machine-gun fire and artillery fire was being sent at us.' Private Telfer, among the RHLI's leading wave, wrote, 'The enemy seemed to hold his fire until we were half-way across the beach and then opened up and we were caught between crossfire'. By the time Private Dury landed, the enemy had fully recovered from the effects of the air strike. He later described his touch-down under fire:

*'As we neared the beach, shells were falling close around us; we learned later that much of this was heavy mortar. Then we ran into MG fire. As we reached the beach and the door opened, we could see the Casino, and right in front was a MG post firing on us.'*

### The Fight for the Casino

On White Beach, the dominating feature facing the Royal Hamilton Light Infantry, immediately behind the seawall, was the large rambling three-storey Casino building. It was strongly fortified by the Germans, with at least one artillery piece in a casemate built into the building on the north-west corner, and pillboxes outside the building, including a particularly strong concrete machine-gun

**A view of the Casino from the beach taken after the battle.**

Northeast
Pillbox

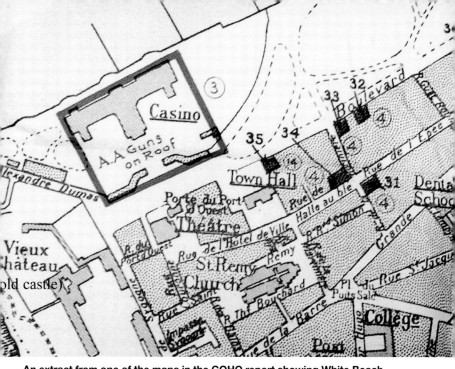

**An extract from one of the maps in the COHQ report showing White Beach and the Casino area.**

casemate near the north-east corner. In addition, riflemen were posted in the tower, and on the Casino's roof an anti-aircraft gun was reported that was 'about the same size as our own Bofors 40-mm.'

Captain Whitaker, commander of the RHLI's Battalion Headquarters Protection Platoon, recalled many years later:

*'The ramp dropped. I led the thirty-odd men of my platoon in a charge about twenty-five yards up the stony beach. We fanned out and flopped down just short of a huge wire obstacle. Bullets flew everywhere. Enemy mortar bombs started to crash down. Around me, men were being hit and bodies were piling up, one on top of the other. It was terrifying... We'd gone in naked with very little fire support.'*

More formally, Captain Whitaker wrote in the RHLI's post-Operation Jubilee report, which was attached to the battalion war diary, that:

*'On landing we were met by heavy enemy fire of all types from the Casino, the buildings and positions along the esplanade and from the headlands on both flanks. The entire battalion was pinned down by the weight of this fire. D Coy, on the west of the Casino,*

*was almost wiped out. In front of us lay three rows of wire, a six-foot wall and 150 yards across the esplanade, Dieppe itself. Many of the Officers and men were killed or wounded in an attempt to cross the beach and scale the wall.'*

The RHLI's difficulties had been observed from craft offshore. The arrangements for bomber or fighter-bomber support to the assault troops were proving to be ponderous and slow. Only a small fraction of requests that made their way up the RAF chain of command were accepted, and the resulting raids were eventually over target as late as eighty minutes after the request. Consequently, despite the biggest air battle going on overhead, Lieutenant Hargraves-Heap aboard one of the flak craft, was ordered in to support the land battle:

*'The ship was manoeuvred close in to the beach, and set a course parallel to the promenade, and about 600 yards off shore with the starboard side facing it. Three Oerlikons and the port battery of pom-poms were detailed to look after the ships' AA defence, whilst the shore was engaged with the starboard pom-poms and one Oerlikon. Three pom-poms were using HE with self-destructive graze fuse, alternate shells having tracer, and the fourth pom-pom used Semi-Armour Piercing. . . We appeared to be having quite a little success with our shelling, and had made a trip up and down the beach twice.'*

With the aid of fire-power such as this, and despite the chaos and heavy casualties on the beach, some of the Hamiltons managed to get Bangalore Torpedoes up to the wire and detonate them. One of the first through the resulting gap was Private Greaves, who charged the pillbox that was causing so much of the trouble: wielding a six-foot Bangalore like a lance, he thrust it into the embrasure and killed or wounded the occupants by detonating it.

With the pillbox neutralised, the RHLI broke into the Casino 'after wire on a sun porch on the front of the building had been cut.' They fought from room to room in the rambling building, with a liberal use of hand grenades. Lance Corporal McDermott from HQ Company was with them in the main rooms of the Casino:

*'I spotted three enemy, and worked my way close enough to throw a grenade, but they didn't seem afraid, because they threw one back which hit me on the foot. I ran about forty feet before it went off, knocking the rifle from my hand. I threw another grenade and followed up, but they had gone, leaving a pool of blood.'*

Among the Hamilton's battle group was Sergeant Hickson of the

One of Dieppe's stongly built and lofty hotel buildings.

attached Royal Canadian Engineers' demolition party. Colonel Stacey reported that:

*'The infantry, assisted by the sappers, who were well equipped with demolition charges, now began to clear the Casino. It was a very large building, and its interior was a maze of rooms and passages of various sizes. Clearing it of enemy snipers was in consequence a long and complicated operation.'*

Sergeant Hickson used his plastic explosive 'mouse-hole' charges to blow holes in the Casino's internal walls to allow the RHLI to clear the building, killing numerous determined enemy infantry in the process. The last enemy bastion to fall was the gun emplacement in the north-west corner of the Casino, which was firing at the approaching tank-landing craft. Sergeant Hickson and his men blasted a way into the casemate. The Canadian report described the action:

*'The casemate was of two storeys, the gun (which was firing upon our ships offshore) being in the upper one. Entrance from the Casino was by a steel door, which was locked. Sgt Hickson blew this door down with a charge, which also killed or stunned the men of the gun-crew. Hickson then entered the emplacement and exploded a one-pound charge on the breach of the gun, in which there was a shell. This presumably destroyed the gun.'*

It had taken over an hour for the RHLI to kill or capture all the

169

Germans in the Casino. Sources indicate that the total number of prisoners taken in the rambling Casino was between twenty-three and thirty. The number of enemy dead was probably double this figure. According to the intelligence log, a report reached General Roberts aboard HMS *Calpe* at 0712 hours that the Casino had been taken. The fight in the close quarters of the Casino was hard, but the days of training in the 'blitzed' buildings of the Isle of White proved to be thoroughly worthwhile for the RHLI. The reflex reactions of trained combat soldiers and the instinctive execution of battle drills carried them forward, in defiance of normal human reaction. In the close-quarter fighting in the Casino, the Germans were outclassed.

However, not all of the Hamiltons were involved in the fight for the Casino. Unable to close with the enemy, others were pinned down on the beach. Sergeant Douglas reported that he:

*'...landed with A Coy and made a dash from the boats to about halfway up the beach. Lieutenant Baisley from then on took us forward over the wall. At this point Lieutenant Baisley was killed. Nobody else tried to go over the wall after that. We did not know exactly where the fire was coming from. The places we fired at were the windows of the tower in the Casino where we could see tracers originating; both rifles and Bren fired into the windows and no more fire was seen from there. We remained on the beach, being pinned down by fire from the high ground to the west of the Casino.'*

Also among those pinned down on the beach, some distance east of the Casino, was Lieutenant Colonel Labatt, along with his Headquarters Company. From here, he 'was able to exercise some direction over the unit by his No. 18 set.' Sergeant Goodman, also of HQ Company, recalled how 'after firing across the seawall with a Bren gun, he was directed by Lieutenant Colonel Labatt to organise men in this vicinity to direct their fire towards the high ground to the west.

**One of 7 *Kompanie's* positions dug into the lawns of the Esplanade and manned by either infantry of the *Wehrmacht* or the *Kriegsmarine*.**

The Eastern Headland, with its concealed enemy positions dominated Red Beach.

## Red Beach

The ground over which the Essex Scottish were to attack was not immediately overlooked by a fortified building like the Casino, but, as described in the Canadian report,

'The beach on which the Essex Scottish landed was completely open and was commanded by the east headland, in which the Germans had weapons sited in caves . . . at a range of only some 400 yards. It was also overlooked by the lofty buildings along the Boulevard de Verdun and by pillboxes on the Esplanade wall, while snipers in the upper parts of the Casino were able to harass the Essex on the beach with fire at longer ranges.'

A considerable volume of fire was directed against the Essex Scottish as they approached the beach 'although the smoke laid from the air must have interfered with that of the guns on the east headland.'

PILLBOXES

A photograph taked after the raid showing some of the pillboxes and caves in the Eastern Headland and harbour all that caused so much trouble.

**German machine gunners in action amongst the rubble.**

Captain Guest led A Company across the beach as a part of the initial assault wave:

*'We touched down 200 yards to the right of where we should have been. We ran across the beach, stumbling on the shingle banks, but we were trapped at the first belt of wire. Through an error, our Bangalore torpedoes had not been allocated to us at Southampton, so Corporal Storr had to struggle to cut the heavy rolls of dannert wire, but it was hopeless. Without Bangalore torpedoes we could have been stuck suffering casualties, but fortunately where we were the wire was not very high above the beach. I took a running jump at the wire and cleared it and the remainder of the men followed me. But by the time we reached a little bit of shelter at the seawall, I had only about 35 out of my 108 men left and the wire on the top of the seawall was impenetrable. Enemy Spandau gunners got anyone who moved up to the wire. There was nothing for it but for us to dig scrapes in the shingle.'*

Elsewhere, the men of the Essex Scottish were more fortunate, but they suffered casualties while they breached and crossed the second wire entanglement. Some of the wounded men collapsed on the wire, thus providing a path across the obstacle for their comrades. Others became caught in the wire as they attempted to cut their way through, such as Private Prince of C Company, who wrote, 'I think the German sniper is a real specialist. They are wonderful shots and go for the officers and NCOs. We found that they were mostly all planted on roofs or in very high buildings.' In addition the Germans directed both mortar and shellfire at the Canadian infantry, along with raking bursts of machine gunfire. Lieutenant Colonel MacRae wrote,

*'There was at this time a great deal of MG fire on the wire obstacles, which caused casualties amongst the troops while crossing said wire. Opinion is that by 0545 hrs, somewhere between 30 and 40% of the Essex Scottish personnel were either killed or wounded.'*

The Commanding Officer started to organise attacks across the Esplanade 'with a view to penetrating into the buildings on the Boulevard de Verdun.' However, with the Germans covering the Esplanade, and with very little fire support, the Canadians were committed to a 'forlorn hope.' Lieutenant Colonel MacRae described the attacks:

*'This crossing attempt was met with intensive gun and mortar fire as well as LMG fire and almost all of the assaulting troops were killed or badly wounded. The companies were reformed and despite the loss of some officers started a second assault under cover of smoke. By this time, some of the 2-inch mortars had been destroyed by enemy fire and the second attack suffered a similar fate to the first... A third attempt on a reduced scale was made to cross the wall and was met by a hail of fire, causing most of the personnel to become casualties.'*

The steep slope of 3-4" pebbles that stopped many of the Calgary Regiment's tanks.

Western Headland

GREEN

WHITE

RED

The enemy continued to mortar the beach and rake it with machine-gun fire from the flanks, causing numerous casualties.

Despite the disaster on the beach, about twelve men from the Essex Scottish under command of Sergeant Major Stapleton succeeded in crossing the Esplanade, and reached the enemy dug in on the lawns and positioned in the buildings beyond. This is the only party of the Essex known to have made such a penetration. According to one witness, 'Stapleton... did a remarkable job of getting forward into the buildings with about twelve men and accounted for a considerable number of enemy in transport and also enemy snipers.' A message in HMS *Calpe's* signal log timed 0610 hours, 'Essex Scot across the beaches and in houses', was interpreted by General Roberts to mean that the whole battalion was across the beach. This misleading information contributed to the commander making an unfortunate decision.

### The Tanks

The German Port Commander, Captain Whan, explained in his report that during training exercises:

> *'I demanded as a final phase that a panzer attempted to advance across the shingle bank on the beach. Within a short while the*

**A Tank Landing Craft disabled having discharged its load of Churchills.**

**One of the track layers that made it up onto the Esplanade.**

*panzer was stuck so firmly that it could no longer be moved. The tracks had to be removed and I remember I made the observation "Now we know that the British can't land here with tanks".'*

Conversely, Canadian trials on what they thought to be similar beaches found that the Churchill could cope with a pebble beach, but none the less, measures for assisting in crossing shingle were developed. However, the combination of enemy fire, steep banks and the large pebbles was to prove an almost insurmountable obstacle for much of the armour.

As the landing-craft tank approached the Red and White beaches, they started to attract enemy fire. Some were hit before they touched down, and others were hit while they were disembarking their load or withdrawing from the beach. Losses among the landing craft and their crews on both Red and White beaches were heavy and made up a significant proportion of the Royal Navy's losses during Operation Jubilee.

It had been planned that the first flight of the Calgary Regiment's Churchills would land with the infantry at 0520 hours, accompanied by engineers who were to construct the timber crib ramps and carry out any demolitions necessary to get the tanks off the beach. The Canadian report explains that:

*'Orders had been issued that the three Churchill tanks on each landing craft would go off first, taking the chance of beach mines (which in fact appear not to have been present), in order to engage the enemy pillboxes. The fighting infantry and beach signal parties, and subsequently the sappers and the infantry working parties, would follow.'*

With the tank-landing craft being fifteen minutes late, the RHLI and Essex Scottish were denied the close support and the cover of the tanks that could have helped get them across the beach. There were further delays once the craft had touched down. For example, LCT 2, which landed near the mole at the east end of the beach, took fifteen minutes to disembark its cargo of three Churchills. This delay was apparently because the tanks' engines had not been warmed up, and all three vehicles stalled on the ramp as they left the landing craft. To confound the Germans' armoured mobility trials that they had conducted on the beach, one of the chespaling Churchill track-layer, trialed during the early summer, worked well. COHQ noted a report that the 'first tank... was seen to proceed up the beach to the Esplanade wall, lay its tracks, climb the wall, jettison the apparatus and move west. The other two tanks followed in its tracks and likewise crossed the wall successfully.'

Landing with the tanks from LCT 2 was Sergeant March, a member of the Black Watch of Canada's mortar detachment, who recalled:

> 'I had a clear view of the tanks as they left the craft. The first tank was hit three or four times but kept going. It went through the wire, but much to my surprise the wire seemed to spring into place again after the weight of the tank had passed over it. After receiving a

**Major Rolfe's damaged armoured car 'Hunter' abandoned on the beach.**

*couple of shots from the French tank which was standing close to the mole along-side of which we landed, our tank opened fire and must have scored a direct hit as the French tank seemed to explode into the air.* [This was the tank concreted into the Mole]. *While this was going on, our second tank 'Cheetah' was on the way out and headed for an enemy pillbox slightly to our left. The Jerries immediately ran from the pillbox and were promptly mowed down by our two Vickers guns, which were being coolly handled by the Essex Scottish. Our third tank 'Cavell', which was towing the scout car 'Hector,' seemed to get stuck half on the beach and half on the landing craft's ramp . . . but a shell burst on the ramp and broke both winch cables. The tank now released rapidly pulled the scout car through the wire and tore through the wall. The last I saw of the scout car it was tearing like hell up Foch Boulevard.'*

Among the scout cars landed by the LCTs were those of the tactical headquarters of the two Canadian brigades: 4 and 6 Infantry Brigades and the Calgary Regiment's HQ. Major Rolfe of the Canadian Signals was aboard 'Hunter,' which was damaged when the Churchill that was towing him reversed into his armoured car, crushing its front. Major Rolfe recalled 'I guess the scout car looked

'Ringer', a churchill Mk II belonging to the Calgary's RHQ.

like a derelict to the enemy, but my radio sets were undamaged, so I operated from the wreck on the beach throughout the operation.' Other radio equipment was brought ashore in hand carts, and Brigadier Southam set up his first HQ in the relative shelter of a crater in the beach, where unfortunately the radios were crushed by a Churchill that was struggling up the shingle slope towards the Casino. The Brigadier joined Major Rolfe in the ruins of his armoured car and was able to pass some information back to *Calpe*.

Most of the Churchills that reached the Esplanade used the path laid by tracklayers. However, a few tanks were able to motor straight up the beach without the aid of cheapsaling, but those that had to manoeuvre on the shingle inevitably became casualties

Canadians watch the action ashore from the bows of an LCT

stranded on the beach. Trooper Pinder, driver of 'Ringer,' one of the Regimental Headquarters tanks (second flight), described the difficulties encountered by many of the Churchills:

> 'Almost immediately we were going up hill, very slowly, then we lost traction and could go no further... we backed down under our own power, swung to the right and started along the beach parallel to the sea in the lowest gear, because of all those damnable round stones that no one mentioned beforehand... A short distance along the beach and there was a "clang" from the front of the tank and we stopped dead, with at least one broken track. Up ahead of us we could see the Casino, and near it a large pillbox which one of our tanks was bouncing 6-pounder shells off with no visible effect. There we were for the rest of the morning, using up our ammunition... Every now and again a mortar bomb would land on the tank, doing us no harm but creating havoc with some of the infantry who were using us for shelter'.

In the shingle by the seawall, other tanks encountered a ditch that the Germans were in the process of digging as a tank obstacle at the time of the raid. Here more than one tank bellied in the pebbles as it attempted to manoeuvre across the bund. Although the shingle caused many of the tank casualties, some of the Churchills were disabled by shells hitting their tracks. However, there are few reports of the heavy Churchill tanks being fully knocked out, as

such guns as were available to German coastal divisions in 1942 were mainly of a small calibre when judged by later standards. Many tanks, disabled in the shingle or hit on the tracks such as 'Ringer,' became in effect pillboxes stranded on the beach firing away at enemy positions until they ran out of ammunition.

Despite the Port Commander's confidence that tanks could not get off the main beach, it is estimated that fifteen of the twenty-seven tanks landed) reached the Esplanade, mainly via points where the shingle was heaped against the seawall: another two drowned in the surf. However, the Calgary Regiment's tank crews

Churchill Mk III 'Cat' knocked out on the lawns of the Esplanade.

who got off the beach and onto the lawns found that concrete anti-tank walls, eight feet high and up to four feet thick, blocked the roads from the Esplanade into the town. The engineer detachments that were supposed to demolish them had not arrived, as they had either become casualties or were pinned down on the beach. Lieutenant Breithaupt, commander of 7 Troop B Squadron, was amongst the tanks that successfully crossed the seawall. He reported that he 'spent the morning circling the Esplanade clearing the infiltration of German snipers into slit trenches and firing at the buildings and cliffs from which we saw enemy fire directed to the beach.'

Lieutenant Bennett landed in his tank, 'Bellicose': 'It was a pretty grim trip as there were so many wounded lying helpless in our path, but we managed to get around them.' Bellicose was able to get off the beach over a bank of shingle near the Casino:

'We made a dash for the Germans who were pinning down our infantry on the near side of the road. To our surprise, they poured out from everywhere, running like hell. Both gunners opened up and we got plenty of them. We even had the pleasure of running down one who tried to dodge us. Then we tried to get into the town behind the Casino but all the streets were very narrow and were blocked with solid concrete walls. We were finally hit properly and our steering was buggered.'

Trooper Clark said:

'The one thing that irks me and has irked me for all these years is that there were several of us up there on the promenade, waiting for the order to advance into the town itself. We were just going round in bloody circles, using up our ammo, being shelled and rolling over people.'

However, Sergeant Dumais, fighting in the area of the Casino, was under fire from enemy position on the seawall, and had cause to be grateful to a roaming tank:

'I was at a loss to know how to stop the enemy fire, but a tank solved the problem: it had seen the firing and engaged the position with cannon and machine gun. The enemy fire stopped immediately.'

Later, another tank scaled the seawall 150 yards from the Casino. Coming to a halt, facing towards the old Castle, it seemed to Dumais that the Churchill had been knocked out.

'It made me mad to see one of our tanks knocked out so easily at a crucial moment. But what was this? The tank cannon was moving *around through 180 degrees and fast too. It was hardly on target when three shots rang out in quick succession. The tank was not dead by a long chalk! The tank stood there, waiting for a reply, and it seemed to be asking How's it feel to get a dose of your own medicine? After about twenty seconds it moved off as if nothing had happened.'*

Overall, the tanks provided significant support to the Essex Scottish and the RHLI, but many of the infantry casualties had been inflicted before the LCTs had arrived and while the cumbersome Churchills were being off-loaded. Too few tanks reached the Esplanade to support too few surviving infantry, and a coordinated engineer effort failed to reached the anti-tank walls.

Major General Roberts.

### The Situation at 0630 Hours

According to the COHQ report, aboard HMS *Calpe*, General Roberts had heard that the enemy's opposition was considerably greater than had been expected he:

'*...realised at 0600 hours that all had not gone according to plan. It was known that the Royal Hamilton Light Infantry and the Essex Scottish Regiment had landed on Red and White Beaches, and that the situation on Green Beach, where the South Saskatchewan Regiment and the Queen's Own Cameron Highlanders of Canada had gone ashore, was*

With poor communications to the troops ashore, glimpses of the action through the smoke could be misinterpreted.

*developing not unfavourably. On the other hand, as far as was then known, no landing had taken place on either of the Yellow Beaches* [No. 3 Commando] *and no word had been received from the Royal Regiment of Canada at Puits* [Blue Beach]. *The LCT carrying the third and fourth wave of tanks were waiting offshore ready to go in, but were not ordered to do so. They subsequently returned to England.'*

General Roberts was unaware of the disaster that had befallen the Essex Scottish and the RHLI. He had interpreted positively such messages as he received, and believed that his battalions were across the beach and the Esplanade and were fighting in the town. From this analysis, he concluded that he should reinforce Red Beach, as

> *'At that time, his main preoccupation was to secure the East headland at all costs, and it seemed to him that more infantry were necessary to achieve this purpose, with the help of the tanks he now knew had got ashore.'*

It was also reported that 'the intensity of the enemy fire on Red Beach had slackened.' Accordingly, he decided to deploy his floating reserve, les Fusiliers Mont-Royal, who were embarked in twenty-six LCP(L)s, under their Commanding Officer, Lieutenant Colonel Menard.

In parallel with General Robert's review, the naval commander Captain Hughes-Hallett was considering the cutting-out operation of the German craft in the harbour to be mounted by HMS *Locust*, the French Chasseurs and the Royal Marine Commando. However, *Locust* had already reported that she had been engaged by heavy enemy fire during an earlier attempt to approach the harbour entrance, and with reports from stricken landing craft coming in to HMS *Calpe*, Hughes-Hallett decided to cancel the cutting-out operation.

At approximately the same time, Commander 302nd Division, *Generalmajor* Hasse came forward to 571 Regiment's Advanced Headquarters on the Western Headland to see for himself the scale of the Allied operation. He later recounted that 'I was contented to see that the attack was mainly halted on the beach or on the lawns and that it appeared that only patrols had penetrated into the town.' Being on the spot and not having to rely on messages and watch-keepers' interpretation of events, of the two land commanders, Hasse had formed the correct picture of the battle's progress.

## Deployment of the Floating Reserve

As the landing craft carrying les Fusiliers Mont Royal approached the beach through the shrouds of smoke laid by the Royal Navy, Sergeant Major Dumais recalled that he could hear '...one continuous roar, unbroken even for a fraction of a second.' Two landing craft were sunk as they broke out of the smoke into the sunlight, and all the other craft were hit in some way before touching down at 0704 hours. However, due to the strong westerly set of the tide, they landed further right on White Beach than had been intended, west of the Casino. The French Canadian soldiers could clearly see that the enemy's fire had not, as reported, 'been subdued.' With a new target on the beach, the German defenders let lose the full force of their fire. So heavy was the expenditure of ammunition that the German post-operational report complained that 571 Regiment had 'expended several days' stocks in less than half a day.' One artillery battery alone fired 1,300 rounds in a matter of four hours.

As was the case with the RHLI and the Essex Scottish, the Fusiliers took what cover they could beneath 'an unscaleable cliff' at the western end of the beach. From here, they made several attempts to move to the flanks: their first attempt was to the right, endeavouring to join up with the South Saskatchewan Regiment, which they knew was attacking the RDF station on the Western Headland from Green Beach; but they found themselves frustrated by machine-gun fire. Next, they attempted to move to the left towards the Casino, but the majority of the men remained pinned down on the beach. The COHQ report recorded that:

> 'Sergeant Dubuc and his men landed opposite the western end of the Casino and succeeded, after a while, in subduing two pill-boxes to their immediate front. The Sergeant and one man then went back to a deserted tank left high and dry by the receding tide. This was the tank that had fallen off the damaged ramp of LCT 159 during the landing. They entered it and got its gun into action against the German defences on the western headland. Having fired off all its ammunition, Sergeant Dubuc left the tank.'

Despite the heavy fire from the headland, Sergeant Major Dumais had reached the Casino, and from his new position spotted three members of his mortar platoon.

> 'I saw them leave the cover of the beach together and make a mad dash across the Esplanade. They were soon separated by their speed. A machine gun opened up on them. Ulrich had got across and

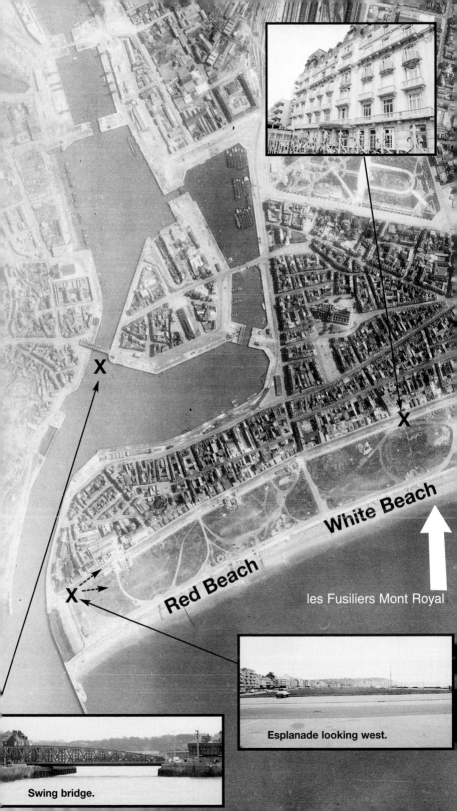

White Beach

Red Beach

les Fusiliers Mont Royal

Esplanade looking west.

Swing bridge.

*hugged the wall out of reach of the Germans. Marechal fell, badly wounded. The machine gun had ripped his belly wide open and he was holding his guts in with both hands. The firing had stopped, so Simard, who could not leave his companion writhing in full view, in mortal pain and yelling for help, jumped up and ran out to him. He picked up his friend and dashed back to cover with him through a renewed hail of bullets. But there was no hope for Marechal and Ulrich dashed back in time to see his friend die.'*

Later the Sergeant Major was able to take his revenge. Peering over a parapet in the Casino, he had a narrow escape from a well-directed burst of *Spandau* fire.

**Rue de Sygogne – the exit fro Esplanade at its western end. Note the concrete wall with it vehicle gate open.**

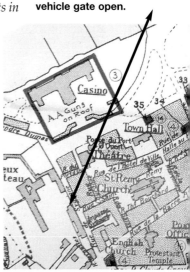

*'I was livid, not scared, just plain mad. The RHLI Corporal had a Bren gun across his knees. "Is this thing working?" "Yes Sir," he replied, "but don't get yourself killed. That guy is good." "So am I!" I retorted. I slapped on a fresh magazine, adjusted the drum, cocked the gun and aligned the muzzle on top of the sandbags. . . I quickly raised myself and the window was right in my sight. I poured a whole magazine of twenty rounds into that window. We had no*

*more trouble from that window!'*
However, despite heroism such as this, the majority of les Fusiliers Mont-Royal were, in the words of the Canadian Official History, 'unable to accomplish anything at all, except to add to the losses being suffered.' As at Puys, the Germans were supplementing the accurate artillery and mortar fire by dropping grenades from the cliff, and amongst the rocks and shell holes, men were becoming casualties. Major Painchaud saw his men lying on the beach. 'They should have taken cover at the bottom of the cliff. Then I realized they were all dead or wounded.' Eventually, Paichaud, the Battalion's Second-in-Command, and Lieutenant Colonel Menard numbered amongst the wounded.

## The Air Battle

> *'Very soon after first light the fighters started their shuttle service over to the French coast. . . The sky was black with them – a very comforting sight.'*

Lieutenant R. Beswick, Landing Craft Flack 4

One of the aims of the raid had been to provoke the *Luftwaffe* into a major air battle. To achieve this, the Allied air forces planned to mount the largest air effort since the Battle of Britain two years earlier. However, even though the RAF put sixty-seven squadrons into the air, including three US squadrons, the range of aircraft at this point in the war meant that their time over target was strictly limited – in some cases, to under ten minutes. For example, the

**An RAF Mustang Squadron in action over Dieppe.**

preponderance of Spitfires (forty-eight squadrons of them) was a problem: though an outstanding defensive fighter, the aircraft, until modified later in the war, had small fuel tanks and a thirsty engine, which limited its endurance in a battle area sixty-five miles across the Channel. However, two aircraft types that later in the war were to play a considerable role in ground attack did well in the raid. Four squadrons of Mustangs (RAF recce variants) flew from Gatwick, while two squadrons of Typhoons operated from Duxford.

During the early phases of the battle, Hurricane bombers and Spitfires attacked the headlands, all the German artillery, anti-aircraft batteries, and the main beach, while Blenheim and Boston aircraft, flying out of Tangmere, dropped smoke bombs. The latter were particularly effective, but despite the heroism of many pilots, the air strike overall lacked sufficient weight or accuracy to be effective. The Germans hit by air strikes were only temporarily suppressed, and recovered quickly once the attacking aircraft had left the area. At this early phase of the battle, the RAF's main opposition was anti-aircraft fire from the guns ranging from small to large that ringed Dieppe. However, by 0700 hours, the *Luftwaffe* were in action.

In 1942, compared with the Allied total of over six hundred aircraft, the Germans had just three hundred fighters in the west, but, in contrast to the RAF, the relatively short distance to their bases for fuel and rearming was a clear force multiplier. The COHQ report described the air battle:

> 'The enemy reacted almost as had been foreseen: at first he did not appear to appreciate the scale of our effort and he used only 25-30 fighters in each sortie. As the day went on, the strength of his sorties increased to between 50-100 aircraft. At first fighter-bombers, and later, when the moves from Holland had been effected, night bombers in increasing numbers were used until all his resources on the Western Front were in action.

> 'Early in the day, enemy air effort was confined entirely to fighters patrolling the area in small numbers. Occasionally, dive attacks on our ships were made from height. The German control merely instructed his aircraft to go to the Dieppe area, where large numbers of British bombers and fighters were operating.'

At about 1000 hours, over five hours after the assault, RAF patrols encountered enemy bombers, who 'it would seem... had not been at a high state of readiness.' Small numbers came into the Dieppe area escorted by *Focke-Wulf* 190 fighters, but 'confined its attentions to our convoy, and did not harass our troops ashore.' Later, German bomber formations of up to fifteen aircraft attacked the Canadians under fighter cover, and it is recorded that 'Reports from pilots indicate that a small number of reserve training bombers were included'. The enemy were clearly throwing all they could into the air battle.

Most of those who survived the raid remembered the aircraft dog-fighting over Dieppe. One commentator wrote that 'the air up above was black with wheeling aircraft.' Another said

> *'Suddenly one of our fighters flashed over our heads with a FW 109 on its tail, with streams of machine gun fire, and we were showered with empty cases – the least of our worries. They both disappeared into the clouds of smoke off the beach.'*

Off Dieppe, the Landing Craft Flak were playing their part in the air battle. Sergeant Cooke of the Royal Marines reported:

> *'Our attention was exclusively concerned with the skies, which suddenly became filled with planes twisting and turning, their machine guns and cannon higher-pitched and more staccato than the guns of the fleet. We opened up with everything that could bear on two of the latest radial-engined FW 190s, and hits were*

**Royal Navy and Royal Marine anti-aircraft gunners in action at Dieppe.**

*registered.'*

There were incidents where the anti-aircraft gunners engaged Allied aircraft, as a result of excitement or misidentification. Sergeant Cooke continued his account:

> *'The pot shots we took at the Mustang roused the skipper's ire. "The next shot at one of those will mean a kick up the arse for someone," he yelled, but he appeared more satisfied when our shells could plainly be seen to mash into the wings of an over-venturesome Focke-Wulf.'*

The planned Allied attack on Abbeville airfield at 1030 hours was 'undoubtedly successful in striking at the enemy's most congested aerodrome at a critical period in the operation.' It considerably reduced the *Luftwaffe's* efforts against the raiding force just as the Allies were starting to withdraw.

Initial claims of a significant Allied air victory abounded in the aftermath of the raid. One headline trumpeted 'Allied Fliers Bag 280 Nazi Planes at Dieppe' and Churchill even told the House of Commons that 'Dieppe was an extremely satisfactory air battle which Fighter Command wish they could repeat every week.' Other newspapers were equally unrestrained, with claims of up to

RAF bombs falling on Abbeville during the course of the raid.

two hundred kills. The reality is that the Germans lost just 48 planes, with some 24 aircraft damaged in air combat. Losses of *Luftwaffe* personnel, including anti-aircraft crew, totalled 104 killed and fifty-eight wounded. Public claims of Allied success (to offset an obvious land reverse?) were also at variance with reality: the Allies certainly lost well over the 106 aircraft that the RAF admitted, although some of the later revisionist historians' claims of over 200 aircraft lost are way off the mark.

## Into the Town

The Casino building, although still the scene of savage fighting, represented a covered route for the Canadians to reach the town from the beach, being just 40 yards from the seafront buildings, rather than 65 yards across the Esplanade's open lawns. It was mainly via the Casino that small groups of Canadians penetrated into the town. Under cover of Bren gun and rifle fire from soldiers of the Fusiliers Mont-Royal and the RHLI, posted in the upper floors, men attempted to cross the fire-swept Boulevard de Verdun. One group of twelve men (all that remained of an RHLI company) was led by Captain Tony Hill in a dash across the Boulevard from the Casino's colonnade into a side street opposite. Once in Rue de Sygogne, they tried unsuccessfully to scale one of the massive concrete anti-tank walls. Looking for an alternative route, they broke into a cinema through a side window and eventually emerged in the town beyond the roadblock. Here they were promptly subjected to rifle fire. Private Liss recalled that

> 'We couldn't see the flash of the rifles and couldn't locate them. It was one of these snipers that got Lance Corporal Sam Harris. He made himself an obvious target by insisting on carrying the Number 18 radio even though the bloody thing didn't work. They were going for commanders and radio operators and before we could get the set off his back he was dead.'

The small engagements were far more evenly balanced, where the Germans, presumably Number 5 *Kompanie*, were in the streets, pressing forward from their positions in the southern part of the town. A surprising number of French people were also out and about. Some seemed to be going about their normal business, but others, who again ignored the warnings to remain impartial during the raid, actively helped the Canadians. Private Gayler reports that,

> 'They came up to us or shouted to us where the Germans were, but on the whole it would have been better if they had stayed out of

*our way because they were giving our positions away as well.'*

Another group, this time French Canadians reached the town. Sergeant Major Dumais, having 'posted every available man at the windows of the Casino to make sure he would make sure we got maximum covering fire,' successfully sprinted across the Boulevarde with six men. They were going to have a go at crossing the anti-tank wall:

*'It was about eight feet high and we were going to have to help each other over. Supporting fire came over our head from the Casino but we lobbed a couple of grenades all the same just in case there were any Germans on the other side. As we climbed over, we could see a small anti-tank gun at the next corner. This came as a surprise; it had not been there before, or we should have seen it from the Casino. Luckily for us, at least two of our Brens were firing at it and the crew had taken cover. We ran towards the gun, three on each side of the street for mutual protection. As we were closing on the gun and getting ready to throw grenades, one of the crew risked a look round the corner. He let out a yell, at which the Germans fled into a street on the right.'*

As the abandoned gun had a round in the chamber, the Canadians turned it on its erstwhile masters on the Western Headland and

**The inland side of the Casino, showing Boulevard de Verdun and the substantial buildings beyond.**

fired, 'only scaring the enemy!' Dumais attempted to lead his group to the St Remy Church, where he was to have used the spire as his mortar platoon HQ and observation post. Again, it was small-arms fire from German infantry in well-concealed positions amongst the buildings that persuaded the redoubtable Sergeant Major Dumais that he should lead his men back to the relative safety of the Casino.

Helped by the fire of one of the roving Churchills, Royal Canadian Engineer Sergeant Hickson, who had earlier played a significant part in clearing the Casino, now led a group of eighteen Canadians across the Boulevarde into the town. He was hoping to reach his objective, the Dieppe telephone exchange, which he was to demolish with his prepared charges. Hickson's group also found that they were up against mounting opposition, and that attempting to move down the roads towards their objective was futile in the face of the growing volume of small-arms fire. Consequently, as their ammunition ran out, they withdrew, 'cutting telephone wires and damaging as much of the militarily useful infrastructure as they could'.

Remarkably, another group of Fusiliers under Sergeant Dubuc fought their way through Dieppe as far as the Bussin du Canada. Here, largely out of ammunition, their luck ran out and they were taken prisoner. Colonel Stacey recounted that:

> 'The party were disarmed, forced to strip to their underwear, and left guarded by one German soldier. This man they overpowered, and the party then began to run, heckled as they went by French civilians unused to seeing semi-naked soldiers in their streets.'

Further to the east on Red Beach, the Essex Scottish had a more difficult task. They had no convenient covered approach to narrow

193

the crossing of the fire-swept lawns of the Esplanade, and, as already noted, only twelve or so men, tossing grenades into enemy trenches, crossed into the town where they reached the Quai du Hable. Here, joined by another small group (probably RHLI), they took up positions in two buildings, and did much damage to German transport and infantry attempting to reinforce the positions along the Esplanade.

### Royal Marines' Attempted Landing

With the commitment of the Fusiliers Mont-Royal and the cancellation of the cutting-out operation, the Royal Marine Commando became, in effect, the last floating reserve. Again, a misleading or misinterpreted series of signals that Major General Roberts received from 0712 hours onwards, led him to believe that the Royal Hamilton Light Infantry had captured the Casino and were ready to move on into the town in force. At the same time, it was apparent to him that, on Red Beach, the enemy troops facing the Essex Scottish were far from subdued. A signal from Red Beach had stated that the enemy's rate of fire was increasing, and two minutes later, it was reported as probably artillery fire. At 0735 hours, the Force Commander:

> '...learnt that a hole had been broken in the Esplanade wall near the Casino and that the tanks had been ordered through by Brigadier Southam... Moreover, it seemed that part, at any rate, of the Western Headland had been captured by the Royal Hamilton Light Infantry, but it was difficult to gauge the exact situation because of the poor visibility. A message was at that time received, asking for bombers to be sent to bomb part of the Western Headland, but this message was almost certainly bogus, for when the sender was asked to identify himself he was unable to do so. Major General Roberts therefore disregarded it.'

Major General Roberts decided to reinforce the apparent success on White Beach. He believed that if the RHLI,

> '... were promptly reinforced, there was a fair chance that the infantry would be able to capture the Western Headland and still break into the town and that it would be possible to carry out many of the demolition tasks before the hour of withdrawal.'

On receipt of orders, Commander Ryder collected as many landing craft as possible and transhipped the Commando into them from the French Chasseur craft. 'This operation took some time and it was not until about 0830 hours that they were ready to begin the

**Sailors watch a destroyer maintaining the smoke screen.**

landing.' The COHQ report records that

> *'Covered by the fire of HMS* Locust, *two Landing Craft Flack, and the Chasseurs, the Royal Marines went inward in their landing craft through a series of smoke screens, which at first afforded them cover. When they emerged from the last of these, they were at once met by the concentrated fire of field guns, light AA guns, mortars, light and heavy machine-guns and small arms. This fire they returned with Bren guns from their landing craft.'*

Captain Deveraux was in one of the leading craft, and described the action in his after-action report:

> *'We had become separated in the smoke, and we were now coming under fire from a coast defence gun and a number of MG positions. About five minutes later the smoke cleared and I saw the beach about twelve feet away. The fire was still intense. There were many prone figures on the beach. Away to the left there were many that appeared dead or wounded... I then saw the CO standing up in*

*the MLC. He was signalling for us to withdraw.'*

However, two craft had already disgorged their cargo of commandos. Lieutenant Smale recorded, after three years in a prisoner-of-war camp, that,

*'The scene on the beach was one of absolute horror and carnage. The whole air was full of the smell of blood and the people who had been blown to pieces. We charged on up the beach towards this knocked-out tank, ...spurred on by the bullets coming towards us.'*

Smale was one of the sixty-six commandos killed or taken prisoner on the beach at Dieppe.

Once he had emerged from the smoke, Lieutenant Colonel Phillipps, Commanding Officer of the Royal Marine Commando, could see how impossible the situation was. 'He realised that, far from being clear of the enemy, White Beach was under very heavy and concentrated fire, and took an immediate decision: to halt the landing – if he could.' In a paragraph inserted in the COHQ report by a very senior officer, Lieutenant Colonel Phillipps' actions are described in detail:

*'Out of the smoke and under heavy fire, the Marines' landing craft were close inshore. Putting on a pair of white gloves so that his hands could be more easily seen, he jumped on to the forward deck of his landing craft and signalled to the remainder to put about and head for the shelter of the smoke-screen. He had scarcely completed this signal when he fell, mortally wounded, but by his action, he undoubtedly saved his men from landing upon a beach swept by a murderous and concentrated fire.'*

On receiving Colonel Phillipps' signal, six of the landing craft turned about and covered their retreat by making smoke. However, before withdrawing, Captain Deveraux rescued the crew of a grounded LCF and then made out to sea 'in a sinking condition, having received a direct hit astern.'

The withdrawal of the Royal Marine Commando was the final confirmation that the assault on Dieppe's main beach had failed. It only remained to extricate as much of the force as possible.

# CHAPTER NINE

# THE WITHDRAWAL AND AFTERMATH

By 0900 hours, having seen the battered landing craft with the Royal Marines aboard coming back through the smoke screen, it was clear to Major General Roberts that there was little prospect of continuing the raid. The Combined Operations HQ report states:

> '...the Military Force Commander was satisfied that the troops on shore were unlikely to gain possession of the headlands to the east and west of Dieppe, ...and that the beaches were still under a fire from them which was steadily increasing. . . At sea, the destroyers were running short of ammunition... and it became increasingly difficult for ships and landing craft to close the beaches.'

The Naval Force Commander, Captain Hughes-Hallett, came to the same conclusion as General Roberts and advised that 'the withdrawal should take place as soon as possible and that no attempt should be made to take away material or tanks'. There was, however, as already mentioned some confusion over the time of the withdrawal, which had unfortunate results at Pourville for the South Saskatchewans and the Cameron Highlanders of Canada. At 0935 hours, the Headquarters aboard HMS *Calpe* had sent the coded signal 'VANQUISH. 1030 hours' to initiate the withdrawal. The COHQ report explains the problem:

> 'It was at first thought that the hour of withdrawal should be 1030 hours, but this was subsequently changed to 1100 hours, for the Royal Air Force Adviser pointed out that an alteration in the hour would upset the time-table to which the Royal Air Force was working and might preclude the possibility of laying the smoke-curtain. The necessary instructions to carry out the withdrawal at 1100 hours as originally arranged were then issued.'

The plan was to send all Commander McClintock's smaller landing craft to the beaches where they had originally landed their troops and to ferry evacuated troops to the LCTs who were to remain

HMS *Calpe* making smoke during Jubilee.

about a mile from the shore. Meanwhile, the destroyers and the Landing Craft Flak 'were to give all possible fire support . . . and all vessels suitably placed were ordered to make smoke'. As there was an onshore breeze, an effective smoke screen was duly made. Also adding to the smoke screen and general fire support were the Churchills of the Calgary Regiment. Twelve of the sixteen tanks that reached the Esplanade returned to the beach leaving four of their number knocked out on the lawns. Given their task of covering the withdrawal, few of the tank crew had any illusion about their chances of evacuation. In the event, only three of the approximately two hundred Calgary Regiment soldiers who landed at Dieppe returned to England.

As indicated above, the Royal Air Force already had plans to cover the evacuation and were already prepared to carry out a series of bombing attacks, mainly on the headlands. Two groups of three Blenheim smoke laying aircraft would augment the Navy's curtain of smoke between the east and west headlands during the period 1100 and 1200 hours. Effective use of smoke played a significant part in the withdrawal plan. One of the post operational conclusions was that:

> 'There is no doubt that these smoke curtains were of great use and their presence made possible the evacuation of a larger number of troops than would otherwise have been the case. They also prevented the infliction of damage to the Naval Craft.'

The smoke however, was a double-edged weapon as it prevented ships engaging targets at the back of Red and White Beaches. Therefore, the ships mainly engaged targets on the headlands, where their fire, as already discussed was least effective.

### The Withdrawal

Events on the other beaches have already been covered in their respective chapters, therefore, this section will concentrate on the withdrawal from Red and White Beaches and the return passage of

**Blenheim smoke laying aircraft.**

the raiding force to the ports of southern England.

The rescheduled withdrawal began at 1106 hours under command of Commander McClintock. Since the code word VANQUISH had been issued, he had been gathering landing craft for the withdrawal into a waiting area about a mile and a half offshore. At the appointed hour, they move in towards the Dieppe beach. As the LCAs broke cover from the smoke, they were hit by heavy fire from the enemy's headland positions and when the boats approached, the waiting infantry ran across the beach. According to Captain Whitaker 'Apart from trying to help the wounded it was every man for himself'. However, some men, mainly wounded, were prepared to cover the withdrawal by staying behind to keep the Germans' heads down. The effect of this was particularly marked on the RHLI on White Beach.

Sergeant Hickson was watching from the cover of the seawall in the area of the Casino and in his personal account described:

*'... a great rush of infantry down from the centre of the beach towards the boats. Instead of scattering they seemed to concentrate on a few craft, and the crowd of men around these craft drew heavy fire.'*

A trio of quotes from anonymous infantryman contained in the COHQ report give a powerful impression of the moment:

*'I made my way out to an LCA, but the first one I came to was hit and I was knocked off it. I was picked up by another which was overcrowded and sinking but another craft came alongside and took off most of the men, leaving the rest of us to bale out until we attracted the attention of a further ship which stopped and took us on board.'*

A second soldier recounted:

*'We got back to the beach and out to an LCA. Before I got in, it pulled out and I hung on to some ropes and was pulled in. A bullet hit me in the arm and knocked me off the rope but I managed to grab the iron bars by the propeller and after it pulled me quite a long way, a couple of people hauled me up over the back and that LCA brought us to Newhaven.'*

Another man recalled:

*'The sea boiled red with the impact of bullets, trashing limbs and gushing wounds. I fought my way into an LCA, ignoring the crew who were inadequate to keep order, and lay gasping in the bottom of the boat as others piled in on top of me. When I could stand up, we were in the smoke bank but still being raked with fire.'*

Most of the craft ferrying the survivors from the beaches to the

LCTs were overloaded, some to the point that they capsized, leaving men mainly without buoyancy aids floundering in the sea. The Essex Scottish on Red Beach, however, received only a handful of craft. Consequently, 392 officers and men waited in vain for rescue, under heavy fire all the while from the Eastern Headland.

Throughout the day, the indomitable Padre John Foote had been calmly ministering to the RHLI's wounded in the scant shelter of the seawall below the Casino. His citation to the Victoria Cross reads,

> 'The calmness of this heroic officer as he walked about collecting the wounded on the fire swept beach will never be forgotten'.

During the withdrawal the Padre helped wounded soldiers of his

battalion down to the craft saw them aboard and then returned back up the beach to help bring down further men. Later he explained:

> 'By the time I had got one wounded soldier slung aboard a boat I was on the deck myself, so the fellow said to me, "Come on" but I said, "No, there are lots of chaplins back in England." I didn't intend to go home because the action wasn't over, my work wasn't done.'

As recorded in his citation 'He refused a final opportunity to leave the shore, choosing to suffer the fate of the men he had ministered to for almost three years'. The *London Gazette* announced that Captain

**Padre John Foote VC.**

**Wounded soldiers disembarking from a landing craft.**

John Foote had been awarded the Victoria Cross for conduct beyond the call of duty on 14 February 1946.

Meanwhile, at the beginning of the withdrawal, 'HMS *Calpe* had made for the western end of Green Beach (Pourville) embarked two landing-craft loads of troops about 1130 hours and then moved off to the main beaches, where she took further troops on board. ML 194 was ordered to round up all the landing craft she could find in the area and send them back into Red and White Beaches. This renewed attempt was met with a hail of fire and the number of casualties amongst the rescued and the rescuers grew appreciably. Consequently, at 1220 hours, Commander McClintock signalled that no further evacuation was feasible. The Military Force Commander, however, asked for still further efforts and the Naval Force Commander replied with the following signal 'If no further evacuation possible, withdraw'. The signal was incorrectly sent or incorrectly decoded and Commander McClintock received it without the first word 'If'. He accordingly brought the evacuation to an end.

Even though officially at an end, Captain Hughes-Hallett personally took HMS *Calpe*, with LCA 185 and LCA 188 on either bow, inshore towards the eastern end of Red Beach for one last look.

*'We engaged German machine gun posts on the breakwater and when about nine cables from the beach, we came under heavy fire. Seeing only wrecked landing craft, I knew that further efforts to evacuate the force would be futile and being ourselves very hotly*

**German machine gunner arriving to reinforce the defenders.**

*engaged, withdrew back into the smoke.'*

Meanwhile, at 1301 hours Major Rolfe, still in the wreck of his armoured car on the beach radioed HMS *Calpe* requesting that they 'Bombard buildings and pillboxes along promenade. Enemy closing in'. The next message recorded by the duty watchkeeper just three minutes later read 'Give us quick support. Enemy closing in on beach. Hurry it up please'.

German communications were still working well and at 1215 hours, *Feldmarshall* von Rundstedt in his Headquarters outside Paris had a clear picture of what was happening at Dieppe and briefed his staff that:

*'The enemy is withdrawing. It is up to us now – and I'm pressing this point – to wipe out as many of the enemy as possible. Drive forward at once! Every available gun barrel must now contribute to the complete destruction of the enemy and the entire front on which he has landed must be cleared in the shortest time.'*

At about this time Captain Hughes-Hallett was asking whether the shallow draft *Locust*, should make one more attempt, 'when the Military Force Commander informed him that he had received a signal stating that most of the troops still left on the main beaches were surrendering'.

The message was passed by a radio operator belonging to C Company, the Essex Scottish's, who 'continued to transmit up to the last moment, the very heavy fire to which he was subjected being clearly heard in the earphones of the telegraphists on board

**Reserve infantry arrive on the smoke shrouded seawall with an anti-tank gun in the background is the Casino pillbox.**

**A German machine gun team moving to the Esplanade during the final stages of the raid.**

the Headquarter Ships'.

Lieutenant Dunlap of the Calgary Regiment described the end.

*'When no more boats were seen to be coming in, the gunfire dropped off and became desultory... We saw troops surrendering in a movement that gradually swept down the beach towards us. Further resistance seemed futile. As the Germans troops appeared in our sector, we raised our hands and gave up.'*

The radio operators on the departing ships sat impotently listened to Major Rolfe reporting that 'They were making a dash for it' and moments later came the final message. 'We are surrendering to the enemy, a mass surrender on Red Beach'. The surrender of the remnants of the RHLI and the Fusiliers Mont-Royal around the Casino and on White Beach took place a few minutes later when German reinforcements started to appear from the Dieppe railway station.

The troops surrendering included Brigadier Southam, commander of 6 Canadian Infantry Brigade. Sadly, he had taken a copy of his operation order ashore in defiance of Major General Robert's instructions and had not destroyed it as the enemy closed in. The resulting insight into Allied capabilities and methods that the Germans were able to glean from it was damaging. However, perhaps the most significant result was that in retaliation for a paragraph requiring the Canadians to bind the hands of German prisoners, the Canadian PoWs spent nearly eighteen months in manacles.

During the final stages of the operation, the destroyer HMS *Berkeley* 'was hit by a heavy bomb dropped by a JU 88 during an encounter with our fighters'. The bomb penetrated the superstructure destroying the bridge and the wardroom, broke the ship's back and flooded the engine and boiler rooms. However, even though she had been abandoned, there was sufficient air trapped in *Berkely's* hull and she remained defiantly afloat. HMS *Albrington* was ordered to sink her in case the floating wreck would fall into the hands of the Germans who would have loudly claimed her as a prize. *Albrington's* first torpedo sank the forward section having detonated just forward or the bridge. The strike of a second torpedo was witnessed by Lieutenant Peter Scott. 'A huge reddish purple burst of smoke and flame belched out of the wreck's magazine and went up into the calm sky in a tall column with a mushroom of dense blackness at its top – an extraordinary and unforgettable sight'.

The Naval Force's withdrawal from the French coast is described in the COHQ report:

> 'On the completion of the evacuation, the craft formed up into convoy approximately four miles to the seaward of Dieppe and were led towards England by the Fernie. The Calpe proceeded to the eastward to pick up a British pilot reported in the sea. She thus moved away from the protection afforded by the concentrated AA

**HMS *Berkley* foundering in the water.**
***Inset:* HMS *Albrington's* torpedo administering the *coup de grace* to HMS *Berkley*.**

*fire of the other ships and sustained two dive bombing attacks in both of which a number of near misses were secured, causing casualties and damage.'*

The report goes on to say that the force's passage back to England 'was uneventful, save for a number of ineffective air attacks'.

*'It proceeded through the western swept channel of the enemy minefield to a point approximately 20 miles from Newhaven where it was joined by HMS* Mackay *and* Blencathra. *These ships escorted the small craft to Newhaven while the* Calpe, *the other destroyers and the* Locust *went direct to Portsmouth having over 550 wounded on board.'*

The coastal and landing craft reached Newhaven without further incident and the destroyers with the *Locust* berthed along side at Portsmouth shortly after midnight.

Sergeant Cooke in charge of the Royal Marines manning the guns on Landing Craft Flack No 5 paints a vivid picture of the events on the passage back to England.

*'On the way back a look at the wardroom and the Mess Deck was sufficient evidence of the sharpness of the action – there was blood and more to spare. The doctor and his assistants worked like Trojans, but their efforts could not prevent the death of several of the wounded survivors we had taken on board. One by one they ware laid out on the deck and a Union Jack found in the pack of a dead Canadian officer was used to cover his body.*

*'One scene will not be forgotten – another Canadian officer Capt Catto, Royal Regt of Canada – having been picked up after some four hours in, the water being helped aboard with his eye shot out quite calmly said "Don't hurry me boys". That was typical of the attitude of the wounded throughout. That was Dieppe as we saw it.'*

## Conclusions

*'The Duke of Wellington said that Waterloo was won on the playing fields of Eaton. I say that D Day was won on the beaches of Dieppe.'*

Admiral Lord Mountbatten

Some commentators have decried the notion that the Dieppe raid provided essential lessons that underpinned the success of the D-Day landings. They say that the lessons had already been learned at Gallipoli and the principals of assaulting a defended coast were already well understood. The fact is that, despite Churchill's tantalizing link with both Galipolli and Dieppe, conditions of warfare had changed and a new generation had to discover what

(Above and below) Canadians march through the streets of Dieppe into three and a half years of captivity.

Canadian wounded being treated in Dieppe after the battle.

was tactically feasible.

Even though information and techniques were clearly developed as a result of the raid, the quickly and so often used public claim that 'vital lessons have been learned' was, during the aftermath of the raid, widely seen to be an attempt to mitigate the public perception of yet another military disaster.

The reality is that the raid was mounted at a point in the war when both, Russia and America, were demanding that the Britain launch a second front in north-west Europe during 1942, in order to relieve pressure on Stalin's armies on the Eastern Front. At the very least, the raid was a reality check and served to concentrate the minds' of Allied planners on the extent of the measures that they must take to breach Hitler's embryonic Atlantic Wall. Gone were plans for Sledgehammer and an unrealistically early return to continental Europe in 1942. The result was that the Western Allies agreed to concentrate on the Mediterranean. In Moscow, Stalin was relieved to see not only German divisions being tied down in France but additional formations being taken from the Eastern Front to strengthen the West against another raid or invasion.

At Dieppe, Combined Operations staff and senior military officers were able to mount the trial landing that they had sought. Remember also Field Marshal Alanbrook's words to Churchill on the eve of the operation:

'No responsible general will be associated with any planning for invasion until we have an operation at least the size of an attack on Dieppe behind us to study and base our plans upon.'

Finally, were the Canadians deliberately sacrificed? Was there a conspiracy? In 1942, after three years of war, the Canadian troops in Britain and their politicians at home, understandably, wanted action and the Dieppe raid was an opportunity to relieve the resulting political and disciplinary pressure. It has to be remembered that the Canadians had a proud military tradition based on their achievements in the Great War where they earned a reputation as being amongst the finest assault troops. Expectations of Canadian performance in battle against the old enemy were high.

Having committed the predominantly Canadian troops and British naval and air forces to the raid, the planning was over restrictive and unrealistically detailed. The force lacked the experience to execute the plan or cope with the inevitable 'events' caused by enemy action and errors in planning or its execution.

The lessons of the raid were numerous and studied in detail, so much so that any list of comparisons between Dieppe and D-Day show a list of self-evident contrasts. Not least amongst the lessons were that it was not a practical proposition to directly attack a heavily defended port area. Consequently, a beach landing on the Normandy coast away from the heaviest of defences was necessary and that a prefabricated port would be necessary to sustain major operations over said open beach. The necessity for special means to overcome coastal defences was starkly obvious to those who had landed on the exposed beaches of Dieppe. Hence D-Day's massive integrated air, sea and land fire plan designed to subdue the defenders, while specially designed armoured vehicles crossed the beach and breached the concrete defences.

While the Allies critically studied the results of the Dieppe raid in detail, the German victor accepted his success far less critically. He came to the conclusion that enemy landings were to be defeated on the beaches and that such landings that succeeded would be limited and driven back by counter-attack. Arguably, causing the enemy to adopt a strategy based on static coastal positions was the greatest result of the Dieppe raid.

**Padre Foote VC marches ahead of the column of prisoners with whom he elected to go into captivity.**

**The Germans buried the Allied dead with full military honours on the hill above Dieppe that they failed to reach.**

# CHAPTER TEN

# DIEPPE TOUR

*'You who are alive on this beach remember that these men died far from home, that others, here and everywhere, might freely enjoy life in God's mercy.'*
ROYAL REGIMENT OF CANADA'S MEMORIAL, BLUE BEACH, PUYS

This tour of Dieppe's 1942 battlefields will take most of a day, the exact duration depending on time spent exploring, relaxing on the attractive beaches or having lunch at one of the many hostelries. A tour is, however, a worthwhile investment of time to gain a fuller understanding of the ground that words, maps and pictures cannot alone convey. The area has changed much since August 1942. There have been the usual impacts of time on the battlefield; new buildings and roads but in addition, the Germans built between the raid and the final liberation of the Dieppe area in August 1944, replacement concrete defences and numerous additional casemates.

Before beginning the tour it is worth making a few points and passing on a couple of warnings:

1. Some of the sites visited and routes are not suitable for heavy vehicles. In some cases, even mini busses will have difficulty. Where this is the case look for the light vehicle only road sign. Partly because of this and the nature of the ground, there is quite a bit of walking to be done in this tour.

2. Beware of theft from vehicles, which seems to be endemic along this coast, even in the remote rural areas. Follow the usual police advice regarding valuables.

3. Please obey traffic and parking regulations. Parking can be difficult at many of the sites at weekends, particularly during high season and on Sunday afternoons.

4. The French authorities formerly ban walking immediately above or bellow the unstable and crumbling chalk cliffs. Certainly, do not be tempted to scramble on cliffs or steep slopes.

5. All the locations described can be seen from public areas, please do not be tempted to stray onto private land.

*The tour follows a chronological route starting with the four flanking operations, followed by visits to the main beaches in Dieppe, finishing at the Canadian Cemetery. This approach requires more driving but it does follow the raid from first to last. The proposed tour can, however, be easily adapted to individual's interests or indeed limitations of time.*

**THE START POINT** for this tour is the main roundabout at the top of the town in Dieppe on the **N27**. Follow the green signs to **Eu** and **Le Treport** around the south of the town past the Hippodrome (racecourse), Neuville-les-Dieppe, the light industrial units and out onto the **D925**. After two miles across open country, turn left onto the **D113E** to **Belleville-sur-Mer**. In the centre of the village, turn right at the Mairie onto the **D113** towards **Berneval-le-Grande**. One hundred and fifty yards after leaving the village turn left onto a narrow winding lane, in the steep sided valley that leads down to Yellow 1 Beach (See page 63). On reaching an open area, park your car. The beach is three hundred yards' walk but there is very little parking and even less room for manoeuvring a car.

The route down to the beach has been improved and the gap in the cliffs enlarged but it is easy to gain an understanding of the difficulties that faced Major Young and his group of commandos, as they struggled up the chalk face to the immediate right of the gap (as seen from the beach).

Once up the cliff, the commandos joined the main track back up to where your car is parked. From the open area, they took the left exit, following the track up to the D113, where they met the French boy on a bicycle. Follow in their footsteps turning left on the road to **Berneval**. In the village turn left past a large floral traffic island and park by the church. It is from the church that Major Young first came under enemy fire.

From here it is best to walk onto **Rue d'General Leclerc**, heading north to the stretch of open country between village and the cliffs, as the village has expanded and the remains of the battery are to be seen in the gardens and are easily missed when in a car. On reaching the edge of the village a large casemate in a field can be seen. This is a part of the post-1942 development that replaced the open gun pits on this site, which were engaged by Major Young and his commandos. Take the track to the left around the village edge until reaching a cross tracks. The commandos followed this route to the right back down to Yellow 1 Beach. However, to return to the transport turn left on the track back into the village. Turn left onto the road and right back onto Rue d'General Leclerc.

From the church, take **Rue Jeanne d'Arc** to Yellow Beach 2 at le **Pettit Berneval**. On entering the village look out for a turning to the right named Rue 3 Commando. Turn down this route and park by the memorials to the British, Canadian, French and American raiders and liberators (photo **A**). It is recommended that visitors walks down the track from the square to the beach via the L'escalier de Berneval. This was the route that the commandos planned to take off the beach. Alternatively, drive back up Rue 3 Commando, across the viaduct and park in the first car park on the left. From here, a steep gully leads down to the beach, marked by a memorial to the commandos (photo **B**) who broke into France at this point. Return to your car and retrace the route through **Berneval-le-Grande** and back onto the **D113** and **Belleville**. Drive through the village and through Bracquemont towards **Puys**. Take the narrow road signposted to the **Plage**.

Park at the sea front. The features in this small area are all easily recognisable from the pictures between pages 102 and 117 of this book. The large memorial, with it moving wording, was amongst the first to be inaugurated by Canadian Premiere Mr Mackenzie-King in 1946. (photo **C**)

Retrace your steps back to the **D 113**. Those who wish to shorten the route and go straight to Red and White Beaches should turn right and follow the road down into the port and cross the left bank via the swing and lift bridges. Those who wish to complete the full tour should turn left back to **Bracquemont** and return to the **D925** via the **D 100** or if in a small vehicle, navigate on the minor roads back to the D 925.

Commando memorial at Quiberville.

Follow the route around the south of Dieppe back to the start point roundabout. Go straight across, following signs to **Petitt Appeville**. Once out of the built up area the Four Winds feature is to the right, note the well concealed post-1942 casemates in the roughs between the golf course fairways. The village of Petitt Appeville at the bottom of the valley was the point of furthest penetration by the Cameron Highlanders of Ottawa from Green Beach (see page 136) to which we will return later in the tour.

Once out of the valley by a mile take the **D55** through **Hautot-sur-Mer**, signposted to **Varengeville**. Join the **D75** and drive

210

**The beach at Quiberville – Orange Two.**

through Varengeville towards **Quiberville**. The view down the length of the beach (Orange II) is little changed from that shown in the pre-war photograph that was used to brief Lord Lovat's No. 4 Commando. Park opposite the first beach huts. A modern memorial stands at he spot where the commandos rushed through the piled coils of dannert wire that stretched the length of the beach (photo **E**). From the road the visitor can see the route taken by Lord Lovat's group along the foot of the Saone Valley.

Retrace your steps back towards Varengeville, watching out for the signs to Phare d'Allie. Park at the road fork by the information sign. This was the Hess Battery observation post and a defended area in it own right, mainly manned by *Kriegsmarine* and *Luftwaffe* personnel. The woods here are a nature reserve, so it is possible to explore the area for signs of battle; trenches and shell holes. The latter are almost certainly exclusively from 1944.

Take the right fork and after a hundred yards, turn right towards **Hotel du Terrace**. This road winds its way through woodland villas to **Porte d'Vasterville** or Orange One Beach (photo **F**). At the T-junction, park in one of the bays provided and walk down the track to the beach. Again the gap has been widened but the scene would be instantly recognisable to Major Mills-Roberts and his

**The easterly of the two gaps at the Porte d' Vasterville or Orange One Beach.**

Memorial to raid and eventual liberation of Berneval.

This stone pillar comemorates where No.3 Commando scaled the cliff.

Merchant Navy memorial.

Royal Regiment of Canada memorial at Puys.

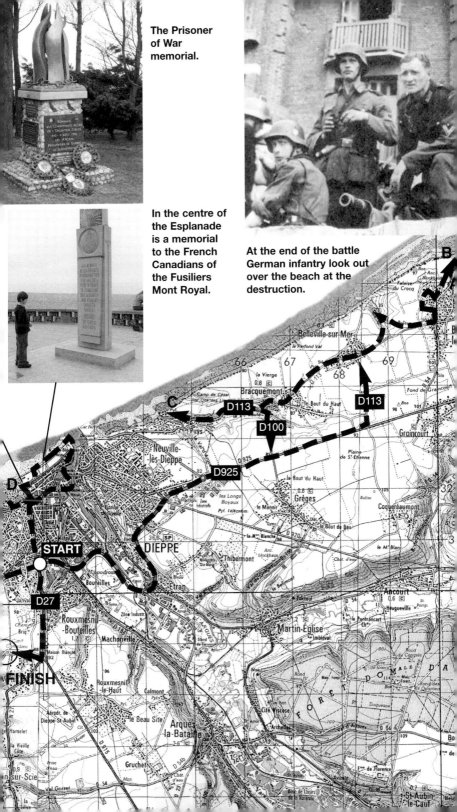

The Prisoner of War memorial.

In the centre of the Esplanade is a memorial to the French Canadians of the Fusiliers Mont Royal.

At the end of the battle German infantry look out over the beach at the destruction.

The author's wife, Kate and children, Jamie, Will and Victoria at the monument to the Royal Regiment of Canada at Puys.

Number One Group (see page 86). By retracing your route back to the vehicle and on through the woods you are more or less taking the same route as Major Mills-Roberts. Sadly the majority of the wood is enclosed by villas and their extensive grounds, which precludes any meaningful expedition through the wood. Drive south from the parking area and stop opposite a modern white villa on the left as the **woods give way to open fields**. It is from here that Major Mills-Roberts gave covering fire to the attack on the battery, which lies amongst the houses about two hundred yards to the front.

Continue on in your car, following the road around to the left at a T-junction. Stop by the Command Post casemates, which are in the gardens on the left, just short of the junction with the main road. There is a plaque commemorating the attack on 19 August 1942 on the casemate that borders the road. The remainder of the battery is also in gardens or private land and little sense of its scale and layout can be gained from the road. If time allows, walking some of the lanes helps. See  map on page 79.

Drive east on the **D75** to **Pourville** (Green Beach) and Dieppe. The wooded feature to the right is the Bois d'Hautot, which gave cover to the Cameron Highlanders in their move inland to Petit Appeville. As one drives down into the Scie Valley and **Pourville** note the hillside across the valley, which is the Four Winds feature, with two small prominent casemates on the crest. Nearer the cliffs, with the road snaking up it is the hill on which the radar station was positioned. Arriving in Pourville, turn of the main sea front road almost immediately and park in the beach side car park. This is the area of Colonel Merrit's Battalion Headquarters and his last stand but the building has been replaced by a modern bar restaurant complex. Across the car park is a memorial featuring the 2nd Canadian Division's badge. At the small church is another pair of memorials raised by the community to the South Saskatchewans and the Cameron

Highlanders. From here it is a short walk to the main South Saskatchewans' memorial and to the Meritt Bridge.

Drive along the beach road and up the zig zags to the **Aire Touristique** and park. From here the view down to the beach can be compared with the intelligence photographs. The problems facing A Company (the radar station) and D Company (the Four Winds feature) can be readily appreciated, as can the ground across the valley, where Cameron Highlanders advanced inland.

**2nd Canadian Division's memorial at Pourville.**

Continue up the road. As one reaches the plateau and the road starts to level out. German trenches that the RDF expert outflanked (see page 113) can be seen on the right but behind the six foot chain link fence on the left various large casemates associated with the radar station can be seen, including a mounted gun. At least one of the radar casemates can be seen broken on the beach below, having fallen from the cliff in the Seventies. The remains of this ruin can be accessed by walking from the either the Pourville or Dieppe beaches. **Watch out for the incoming tide**.

Drive on past the golf course and the college and look out for the left turn signposted **Chateau Musee** onto **Avenue de l'Esplanade**. Park in the designated bays at the cliff edge. From here, the classic view (see page 146) over the main Dieppe beach and the Esplanade dispels any doubts about the feasibility of an operation to attack a defended port with scant fire support.

**One of the monuments below the Vieux château.**

To reach Red and White Beaches, retrace your steps back to the road and continue down into the town and follow the one way system, then the **Toutes Directions** followed by the Plage sign. This takes the visitor past the harbour's Avant Port across which the Swing Bridge can be seen. Note the number and variety of restaurants in this area and the number of casemates built into the cliff and the prominent church on the Eastern Headland.

Arriving on the **Esplanade**, park where you can. Second to appreciating the view from the Western Headland, no visit

**The Essex Scottish memorial on Red Beach.**

to Dieppe is complete without a walk along the beach, the Esplanade and the lawns. Do not exclude the small garden at the foot of the Vieux Chateau which contains, amongst others, memorials to the prisoners of war and the naval forces (photo **D**). The tranquillity of this spot is in contrast with the hurly burly that surrounds the memorials on the main Esplanade.

The tour of the Dieppe battlefields concludes at the Common Wealth War Graves Commission Canadian Cemetery. To reach the cemetery follow the one-way system off the Esplanade under the walls of the Vieux Chateau and at the junction with the main road, **turn right uphill**. At the second roundabout take the minor road to the west, this is signposted **Canadiane Cimiterie** on a local road sign rather than on the usual green and white CWGC sign. Once off the roundabout follow the normal CWGC signs to the cemetery.

The cemetery contains nearly nine hundred graves of soldiers, sailors and airmen. These are mainly but not exclusively, from 1940, the 1942 raid and the 1944 campaign. The vast

RED

WHITE

Site of casino

**The classic view of the Esplanade from the western headland.**

majority are Canadians of 2nd Division; some 707 identified and unknown graves. Other graves represent virtually every service and branch of the force assembled under Combined Operations for the raid. This quiet hill top spot is a good point to contemplate the events that culminated in the raid and the deaths of so many men. It also makes a fitting end to the tour.

## Additional Visits

Many of the wounded soldiers who were evacuated from the beach and subsequently died of their wounds are buried in the Brookwood CWGC military cemetery west of London. This showpiece cemetery is well worth a visit.

The second place to visit on the UK side of the Channel is the Newhaven Museum, which has a display relating to Operation Jubilee. This museum should be visited if at all possible by those travelling on the Newhaven to Dieppe ferry service.

**The cemetery on the outskirts of town principally contains casualties of the Raid.**

# ORDER OF BATTLE

**Naval Forces** – Captain J Hughes-Hallett RN

**Destroyers:**
HMS *Calpe* – Headquarters Ship 1.
HMS *Fernie* – Headquarters Ship 2.
HMS *Garth*
HMS *Berkeley*
HMS *Bleasdale*
HMS *Brocklesby*
ORP (Polish) *Slazak*

**Sloops and Gunboats:**
HMS *Alresford*
HMS *Locust*

**9th and 13th Minesweeper Flotilla**

**Landing Ships Infantry:**
HMS *Glengyle* – LSI(Large)
HMS *Queen Emma* – LSI(Medium)
HMS *Princess Beatrix* – LSI(M)
HMS *Prince Charles* – LSI(Small)
HMS *Prince Albert* – LSI(S)
HMS *Invicta* – LSI(S)
HMS *Prince Leopold* – LSI(Hand Hoisting)
HMS *Duke of Wellington* – LSI(HH)

**Landing Craft:**
1st, 2nd, 4th, 5th, 6th 7th and 24th Landing Craft Flotilla
1st Landing Craft Flotilla
2nd and 4th Landing Craft Tank Flotilla
Escort Flotilla
Motor Gunboats x 12
Steam Gunboats x 4
Motor Launch x 21
Chasseurs x 7 mainly Free French

**Land Forces** – Major General JH Roberts MC

Headquarters 2nd Canadian Division (Embarked on HMS *Calpe* and HMS *Fernie*)
2nd Canadian Division Canadian Corps of Signals
2nd Canadian Division Intelligence Section

2nd Canadian Division Field Security Section

Headquarters 4th Canadian Infantry Brigade
J Section 2nd Canadian Division Canadian Corps of Signals
Royal Regiment of Canada
Royal Hamilton Light Infantry
Essex Scottish

Headquarters 6th Canadian Infantry Brigade
L Section 2nd Canadian Division Canadian Corps of Signals

Fusiliers Mont Royal
Cameron Highlanders of Canada
South Saskatchewan

Black Watch of Canada (1 company)
Calgary Highlanders (2 sections)

Divisional Troops and others (mainly detachments)
14th Canadian Tank Battalion (The Calgary Regiment) B and C Squadrons
8th Canadian Reconnaissance Regiment (14th Hussars)
Royal Canadian Artillery and BEF Forward Observation Officer parties
7th Field Company, Royal Canadian Engineers
Toronto Scottish (Machine Gun Battalion)
2nd Canadian Division Royal Canadian Service Corps
2nd Canadian Light Field Ambulance
2nd Canadian Division Royal Canadian Ordnance Corps
2nd Canadian Division Canadian Provost Corps
2nd Canadian Division Canadian Intelligence Corps
GHQ Reconnaissance Regiment

Commando Forces (Under command 2nd Canadian Division)
Number 3 Commando
Number 4 Commando

A Commando Royal Marines
Detachment 10 Inter-Allied
Commando
Detachment 1st US Rangers

**Air Forces** – Air Marshal T Leigh-
Mallory CB DSO

*Kenley Sector*
    Kenley – 4 Squadrons
    Redhill – 3 Squadrons
*Northolt Sector*
    Northolt – 2 Squadrons
    Heston – 2 Squadrons
    Redhill – 1 Squadron
*Tangmere Sector*
    Merston – 2 Squadrons
    W. Hampnett – 1 Squadron
    Thorney Island – 2 Squadrons
    Shoreham – 2 Squadrons
    Friston – 2 Squadrons
    Ford – 4 Squadrons (2 x
      Hurribombers & 2 Day
      Bomber)
    Thruxton – 1 Squadron
    (Boston aircraft for smoke)

*Debden Sector*
    Gravesend – 3 Squadrons
    Hawkinge – 2 Squadrons

*North Weald Sector*
    Southend – 2 Squadrons
    Manston – 4 Squadrons

*Hornchurch Sector*
    Hornchurch – 3 Squadrons
    Fairlop – 2 Squadrons
    W./ Malling – 4 Squadrons

*Biggin Hill Sector*
    Biggin Hill – 3 Squadrons
    Lympne – 2 Squadrons
    Eastchurch – 2 Squadrons
    Hawkinge – 1 Squadron

Army Co-operation Squadrons
    Gatwick – 3 Squadrons
    Thruxton 2 (Smoke laying
      aircraft)

# Appendix 1

## Victoria Cross Citations

ANTHONY PORTEOUS, R.A.
*Captain (Temporary Major), 73033, Royal Artillery*
**Victoria Cross**
War Office - 2nd October 1942.

The KING has been graciously pleased to approve the award of the VICTORIA CROSS to:

Captain (temporary Major) Patrick Anthony PORTEOUS (73033), Royal Regiment of Artillery (Fleet, Hants.).

At Dieppe on the 19th August, 1942, Major Porteous was detailed to act as Liaison Officer between the two detachments whose task was to assault the heavy coast defence guns.

In the initial assault, Major Porteous, working with the smaller of the two detachments, was shot at close range through the hand, the bullet passing through his palm and entering his upper arm.

Undaunted, Major Porteous closed with his assailant, succeeded in disarming him and killed him with his own bayonet thereby saving the life of a British Sergeant on whom the German had turned his aim.

In the meantime, the larger detachment was held up, and the officer leading this detachment was killed and the Troop Sergeant-Major fell seriously wounded. Almost immediately afterwards the only other officer of the detachment was also killed.

Major Porteous, without hesitation and in the face of a withering fire, dashed across the open ground to take over the command of this detachment. Rallying them, he led them in a charge, which carried the German position at the point of the bayonet, and was severely wounded for the second time. Though shot through the thigh he continued to the final objective where he eventually collapsed from loss of blood after the last of the guns had been destroyed.

Major Porteous's most gallant conduct, his brilliant leadership and tenacious devotion to a duty, which was supplementary to the role originally assigned to him, was an inspiration to the whole detachment.

## LIEUT.-COL. CHARLES CECIL INGERSOLL MERRITT
*South Saskatchewan Regiment*
### Victoria Cross
Department of National Defence, Ottawa.                     *2nd October 1942.*
### THE CANADIAN ARMY

The KING has been graciously pleased to approve the award of The VICTORIA CROSS to:

Lieutenant-Colonel Charles Cecil Ingersoll MERRITT, The South Saskatchewan Regiment.

For matchless gallantry and inspiring leadership whilst commanding his battalion during the Dieppe raid an the 19th August 1942. From the point of landing, his unit's advance had to be made across a bridge in Pourville which was swept by very heavy machine-gun, mortar and artillery fire: the first parties were mostly destroyed and the bridge thickly covered by their bodies. A daring lead was required; waving his helmet, Lieutenant-Colonel Merritt rushed forward shouting "Come on over! There's nothing to worry about here." He thus personally led the survivors of at least four parties m turn across the bridge. Quickly organizing these, he led them forward and when held up by enemy pillboxes he again headed rushes which succeeded in clearing them. In one case, he himself destroyed the occupants of the post by throwing grenades into it. After several of his runners became casualties, he himself kept contact with his different positions.

Although twice wounded Lieutenant-Colonel Merritt continued to direct the unit's operations with great vigour and determination and while organizing the withdrawal he stalked a sniper with a Bren gun and silenced him. He then coolly gave orders for the

departure and announced his intention to hold off and "get even with" the enemy. When last seen he was collecting Bren and Tommy guns and preparing a defensive position which successfully covered the withdrawal from the beach.

To this Commanding Officer's personal daring, the success of unit's operations and the safe re-embarkation of a large portion of it were chiefly due. Lieutenant-Colonel Merritt is now reported to be a Prisoner of War.

HONORARY CAPTAIN JOHN WEIR FOOTE
*Canadian Chaplain Services Royal Hamilton Light Infantry*
**Victoria Cross**

Department of National Defence, Ottawa. *14th February 1946.*

**THE CANADIAN ARMY**

The KING has been graciously pleased to approve the award of the VICTORIA CROSS to:

Honorary Captain John Weir FOOTE, Canadian Chaplain Services.

At Dieppe, on 19th August, 1942, Honorary Captain Foote, Canadian Chaplain Services, was Regimental Chaplain with the Royal Hamilton Light Infantry. Upon landing on the beach under heavy fire he attached himself to the Regimental Aid Post which had been set up in a slight depression on the beach, but which was only sufficient to give cover to men lying down. During the subsequent period of approximately eight hours, while the action continued, this officer not only assisted the Regimental Medical Officer in ministering to the wounded in the Regimental Aid Post, but time and again left this shelter to inject morphine, give first-aid and carry wounded personnel from the open beach to the Regimental Aid Post. On these occasions, with utter disregard for his personal safety Honorary Captain Foote exposed himself to an inferno of fire and saved many lives by his gallant efforts. During the action, as the tide went out, the Regimental Aid post was moved to the shelter of a stranded landing craft. Honorary Captain Foote continued tirelessly and courageously to carry wounded men from the exposed beach to the cover of the landing craft. He also removed wounded from inside the landing craft when ammunition had been set on fire by enemy shells. When landing craft appeared he carried wounded from the Regimental Aid Post to the landing craft through very heavy fire.

On several occasions, this officer had the opportunity to embark but returned to the beach as his chief concern was the care and evacuation of the wounded. He refused a final opportunity to leave the shore, choosing to suffer the fate of the men he had ministered to for over three years.

Honorary Captain Foote personally saved many lives by his efforts and his example inspired all around him. Those who observed him state that the calmness of this heroic officer as he walked about, collecting the wounded on the fire-swept beach will never be forgotten.

# Appendix 2

## Advice to Visitors

Preparation and planning are important prerequisites for an enjoyable and successful tour. This section aims to give some advice to those who are travelling to France for the first time and acts as a checklist for the more seasoned traveller.

**Travel Documentation**
UK and European Union citizens are required to carry passports when travelling to France. However, many non-EU citizens will require a visa to visit France – check with the French Embassy in your country of origin before travelling.

**Travel to Dieppe**

Most visitors travelling to the Northern France do so by car. However, with Dieppe's direct access by ferry, an increasing number of visitors are cycling around the battlefields. Whatever the visitors' mode of travel around the Dieppe area, a journey originating in the UK has to cross the Channel. A wide range of options available. The most convenient ferry service is the route from Newhaven direct to Dieppe. The service, however, only typically operates from around Easter to the end of October. Delivering the visitor to Dieppe reduces continental driving and has the benefit of the view enjoyed by those who took part in the raid. An hour to the west is le Havre, which is served by ferries from Portsmouth. Choice for most visitors depends on the convenience of the sailing times and, of course, relative costs. To the east of Dieppe are the shorter, and consequently cheaper, crossings in the Calais area and or those who dislike ferries there is the Channel Tunnel, but this option, though quicker, is usually more expensive. From Calais, Dieppe can be easily reached via the autoroute in two hours but bear in mind tolls cost up to £5 each way. It is worth checking out all the options available and make your selection of routes based on UK travel, ferry times and cost. French law requires you to carry a full driving licence and a vehicle registration document. Do not forget a GB sticker if you do not have EU number plates with the blue national identifier square.

**Insurance**

It is important to check that you are properly insured to travel to France. Firstly, check with your insurance broker to ensure that you are covered for driving outside the UK and, secondly, make sure you have health cover. Form E111, available from main post offices, grants the bearer reciprocal treatment rights in France but, even so, the visitor should consider a comprehensive package of travel insurance. Such packages are available from a broker or travel agent. It is a legal requirement for a driver to carry a valid certificate of motor insurance. Be warned that without insurance, repatriating the sick or injured is very expensive, as is return of vehicles.

**Accommodation**

There is a very wide range of hotels in the Dieppe area, ranging from five star to Chambres d'hotel, however, the latter are not as numerous as in Lower Normandy. The usual Ibis, Campaniele, Mercure chain hotels are to be found on the southern edge of town astride the D 915. Up to date contact details are available from the French Tourist Office, 178 Picadilly, London W1V 0AL (01891 244 123). Further details of accommodation and travel amenities are available from the office of Dieppe Tourisme. To telephone from the UK dial 0033, drop the 0 necessary for ringing within France.

**Maps**

Good maps are an essential prerequisite to a successful battlefield visit. Best of all is a combination of contemporary and modern maps. The Battleground series of course, provides a variety of maps. However, a number of modern map series are available in both the UK and in Dieppe. Most readily available in both countries are the Michelin 1:200,000 Yellow Series. Better still are the Institut Geographique National (IGN) 1:100,000 Serie Vert (Green Series) maps. Normally only available in the UK at a specialist map shop they can, however, be procured as a special order through high street bookshops such as Waterstones. The Series Vert maps have the advantage of showing contours and other details such as unmade roads and tracks. The most detailed maps, readily available in France, are the IGN Serie Bleue in 1:25,000 scale. The map covering Dieppe can normally be found in the tourist shops in Dieppe. However, if you are planning your tour well in advance, large retailers in the UK can order Serie Bleue maps, given sufficient notice. The London map retailer Stamfords, provides a quick and easy method of ordering IGN maps on line.

**Courtesy**
Much of the area where the flanking attacks took place is open farmland but many of the villages in the area have expanded and the German strong points have in some cases been built over, around or enclosed. Please respect private property in both open country and villages, particularly avoiding driving on unmade up farm tracks and entering non-public areas. Adequate views of the scene of the action can be gained from public land rights of way. In all cases, please be careful not to block roads by careless car parking. The people of Northern France extend a genuine welcome to those who come to honour the memory of those who raided Dieppe in 1942. To preserve this welcome please respect the local people and their property.

# Bibliography

*Dieppe Revisited – A Documentary Investigation.* John P Campbell. Frank Cass & Co Ltd 1993
*Dieppe 1943 – The Jubilee Disaster.* Ronald Atkin. Mac Millan 1980
*Clash by Night.* Brigadier Derek Mills-Roberts William Kimber 1956
*The Commandos at Dieppe.* Will Fowler. Harper Collins 2002
*Combined Operations.* HMSO 1943
*Unauthorised Action – Mountbatten and the Dieppe Raid.* Brian Loring Villa Oxford University Press 1989
*Dieppe Tragedy to Triumph.* Brigadier Denis and Shelagh Whitaker Leo Cooper 1992

# INDEX